ALAN HEATON

LOOK WHAT CHEMISTRY DID FOR ME

A life in and out of the lab

ALAN HEATON

LOOK WHAT CHEMISTRY DID FOR ME

A life in and out of the lab

MEREO
Cirencester

Mereo Books

1A The Wool Market Dyer Street Cirencester Gloucestershire GL7 2PR
An imprint of Memoirs Publishing www.mereobooks.com

Look What Chemistry Did For Me: 978-1-86151-815-6

First published in Great Britain in 2017
by Mereo Books, an imprint of Memoirs Publishing

Copyright ©2017

Alan Heaton has asserted his right under the Copyright Designs and Patents Act 1988 to be identified as the author of this work.

A CIP catalogue record for this book is available from the British Library.

This book is sold subject to the condition that it shall not by way of trade or otherwise be lent, resold, hired out or otherwise circulated without the publisher's prior consent in any form of binding or cover, other than that in which it is published and without a similar condition, including this condition being imposed on the subsequent purchaser.

The address for Memoirs Publishing Group Limited can be found at
www.memoirspublishing.com

The Memoirs Publishing Group Ltd Reg. No. 7834348

Design and artwork - Ray Lipscombe

The Memoirs Publishing Group supports both The Forest Stewardship Council® (FSC®) and the PEFC® leading international forest-certification organisations. Our books carrying both the FSC label and the PEFC® and are printed on FSC®-certified paper. FSC® is the only forest-certification scheme supported by the leading environmental organisations including Greenpeace. Our paper procurement policy can be found at www.memoirspublishing.com/environment

Typeset in 12/18pt Century Schoolbook
by Wiltshire Associates Publisher Services Ltd. Printed and bound in Great Britain
by Printondemand-Worldwide, Peterborough PE2 6XD

I dedicate this book to my wife Joy, for all her love and support and for sharing with me the bringing up of our special family. As my mother put it so well: "Joy is the glue that holds our family together".

It is also dedicated to the memory of my mother, for all her inspiration and support.

CONTENTS

Introduction

Chapter 1	The early years, and the first television in our road	1
Chapter 2	Grammar school – academic failure and sports star	5
Chapter 3	Time to get a job	11
Chapter 4	Study, more study and getting married	16
Chapter 5	Carrying out research funded by NASA	24
Chapter 6	Starting an academic career	35
Chapter 7	Promoting chemistry to young people, and teaching in Malaysia	46
Chapter 8	Tutoring for the Open University	57
Chapter 9	Becoming a published author	69
Chapter 10	Industrial Fellowship at ICI	80
Chapter 11	My contributions to the Learned Societies in Chemistry	88
Chapter 12	Drama on a mountain peak	97
Chapter 13	Retirement, and setting up a BSc course in Oman	106
Chapter 14	The Sultanate of Muscat and Oman – a country like no other	124
Chapter 15	How chemistry transforms our lives	133
Chapter 16	Looking back on a full life	156

INTRODUCTION

Do you believe that the chemical industry has had a negative effect on our lives? If you do, is that view a result of some of the sensational stories in newspapers about one of the rare chemical spillages or other disasters? Have you any idea what life would be like without the contribution of the science of chemistry and the chemical industry?

If you feel this way, prepare to be surprised, and perhaps to have your views changed.

The following is the story of a life spent largely in the world of chemistry, mainly as a college or university-level teacher. It is also the story of an ordinary boy, a child of the war years, who rose from an unpromising start, leaving school at 16, to become more successful and fulfilled in a career than he had ever imagined possible.

CHAPTER 1

THE EARLY YEARS, AND THE FIRST TELEVISION IN OUR ROAD

I was born on the 19th June 1942, in the middle of World War 2, at our house in Breckon Hill Road, Middlesbrough. My birth may have been hastened because the previous evening my mother had sat on the steps of Middlesbrough Town Hall watching German aircraft bombing the docks and lighting up the sky. Later I was christened Charles Alan Heaton, the first name after my paternal grandfather and the second after my father.

My mother, Enid Olga Heaton (née Reed), came from Middlesbrough and was a nurse. She had met my father, John Arthur Alan Heaton, when they were both assigned to an air raid shelter and first aid post in a district of the town called North Ormesby, she as the nurse and he as the police officer. He was born and brought up in Rudheath near Northwich in Cheshire, where his father spent all his life working for the giant chemical company ICI. I still proudly own the carriage clock which the company presented to him after 25 years' service. My father was to go on and serve in the Middlesbrough police force for even longer – 30 years.

On 26th November 1944, my brother Russell was born.

I have little recollection of my very early years except for one really traumatic event. At about five years old I was standing in front of our coal fire keeping warm when a spark or a hot coal set my pyjamas alight. Although my parents reacted quickly to put out the flames, my right leg was badly burned. I spent several weeks in hospital and remember the terrible pain each day when the dressing was changed. Even today I still have the scar from ankle to knee, an area where no hair ever regrew.

A couple of years later we moved to Downside Road in Acklam, a suburb on the outskirts of Middlesbrough. This was very handy for Whinney Banks Junior School, which I attended and where I played for the school football team. There was also a very large area of grassland behind our houses where we could play football or cricket every night after school. The most notable events at this time were the conquering of Mount Everest by Hillary and Tensing and the coronation of Queen Elizabeth the Second in June 1953. All the neighbours, particularly the mums, came to our house to watch the ceremony since we had the only television set in the road – black and white of course.

In 1953 I passed the Eleven Plus exam, which qualified me to go to Acklam Hall Grammar School. On hearing this news I cycled several miles to the clinic where my mother worked in the centre of Middlesbrough to tell her the good news. But some weeks later I was dismayed to learn that I would not be going to that grammar school like most of my friends. It was only a mile from my home, but instead I was assigned to Middlesbrough High School in the centre of town. This meant a cycle ride of several miles there and the same back in the afternoon.

A couple of years later we moved to a house in Ashford Avenue, just a few streets away. This property backed on to allotments, which we referred to as the 'pig alleys', and for a short time my father raised a few pigs. After the butcher had dealt with one I well remember it hanging in our little bedroom for a few weeks to 'cure'.

My father bought an early Ford Anglia, whose registration I still remember – ADC 477. His mother was horrified at the cost of it, but it did enable us to visit my paternal grandparents in Northwich during the school holidays. Since they lived in Cheshire each journey was a major undertaking and probably took six to seven hours;

there were no motorways in those days over the Pennines. Nowadays the journey can be done in two and a half hours, assuming no traffic delays.

There was a small tributary of the River Tees a few hundred yards away from our house, and I look back with horror at the times in the summer that we swam in it. It was terribly polluted, but maybe the 'nasties' in it built up our immunity and helped us to enjoy good health. Tragically a youngster went missing in it one day and I remember police divers (colleagues of my father) changing at our house, and eventually recovering the body.

For my brother and me these were happy times growing up with parents who fully supported what we wanted to do. They both worked full time, so we had a young woman living in to help look after us and help run the house. This enabled them to purchase a caravan which they sited at Swainby, at the foot of the North Yorkshire Moors, and we spent many enjoyable weekends and holidays there.

CHAPTER 2

GRAMMAR SCHOOL - ACADEMIC FAILURE AND SPORTS STAR

All my spare time was spent playing soccer with my friends, but I also had a paper round before and after school, which, ironically, covered the houses near Acklam Hall Grammar School. One morning I fell out with another paper boy and in a subsequent fight he swung me into the corner of a wall. I cycled home with blood pouring from a wound above my eye and mum had to drive me to hospital to have it stitched.

This love of sport and all the practice and skills development were to reap rich rewards at Middlesbrough High School. In my early years I represented the school in the town athletics championships. I became the 100 metres champion and also came second in both the shot put and relay. I was a member, and occasionally captain, of the school cricket team and we played schools as far away as Newcastle and Scarborough. The matches only lasted around three hours, with both teams needing to bat, and I was very proud of scoring 47 in one match.

In my final year a bizarre incident occurred early in the season. I was fielding at mid-off and had to move several yards to make a catch. Unfortunately my second-hand cricket boots had lost most of their spikes and I was slipping, so I had to dive full length and make the catch, so it looked quite spectacular. My 'reward' from the captain was to be placed at the very dangerous silly mid-off position, right near the batsman, in every match. This was to come up again in 2014 when a new member of my crown green bowls club in Heswall came up to me and said that he was from Middlesbrough and he remembered me being an excellent cricketer playing for the school team, as he also had done, although he is a few years older than me.

I also won the school tennis tournament in my final year, beating a classmate in the final. He was a better player than me and a member of a tennis club but with my 'never say die' attitude, I just kept the rallies going until he made mistakes, and he made many.

My greatest achievements were in rugby. I remember playing in inter-house matches at our school and on one occasion, when I was 13, being asked to play in the under-15 match. Playing on the wing, I was directly up against a member of the school under-15 team. Of course, at that age two years makes a big difference in size and weight. He ran straight at me, but I was determined that he was not getting past me and made a textbook tackle, bringing him down. I was really proud of this, but my arm and shoulder ached for a week afterwards.

Throughout my time I captained my year school team and my crowning glory was at under-15 level. Here I was selected to play for my county of North Yorkshire in my key position of stand-off, or flyhalf, probably the most important position in any team.

Our first match was away to County Durham, which had a lot more schools and players to choose from. Early on I made a great break and found I had only their fullback to beat. He was big and I tried to run around him, but he tackled me. If I had been more experienced I would have realised that chipping the ball over him would have certainly led to a try. After that they pulled away to win 24-6. Next we were at home to Northumberland, but we lost 9-3, although I did kick the penalty for our points.

For the final match we travelled over the Pennines to Penrith to face Cumbria. It was raining heavily and the pitch was a quagmire, but we managed to prevail, with my penalty kick giving us a 3-0 win. Our coach kept from us until after the match the news that Cumbria had had handsome wins over the other two counties.

At 16 I turned out for the school first team, which covered 16-18 year olds. We had some notable successes, including being the first team in three years to beat Coatham Grammar School in Redcar. I made the breaks and passes for our speedster to race in for three tries in our 9-3 victory.

On the academic front it was very different, and I remember our English teacher, Colonel Platt, calling me a 'blithering idiot' in front of the whole class when I was reading a passage to them and said 'lions' instead of 'loins'. There was a teacher who had difficulty controlling us and someone put a snowball on his stool, which he duly sat on. Another teacher, who was just the opposite, threatened at one stage to 'whack' the lot of us. When we laughed he got out a sandshoe (trainer) and every member of the class of around 30 boys had to bend over in turn whilst he smacked our bottoms with it.

The other teacher I remember was Mr Metcalfe, our chemistry teacher, because in the lab one day a pupil went up to him, stuck a test tube under his nose and said "is this smell chlorine?" Unfortunately it was, and the teacher was taken ill for a while.

I would leave with just four 'O' Level GCEs (now GCSEs), and not very good grades either. However, before that two important things happened. In early June 1958, when the GCE 'O' and 'A' level exams had finished, the school organised a trip to the world's first nuclear power plant, Calder Hall, situated at what is now known as Sellafield in Cumbria. Although this was for sixth formers, there must have been a vacancy, because I was the only fifth former invited. It involved an overnight stay at the youth hostel in Boot. It was a fascinating tour. Little did I know that I would return to the site many years later when I placed students there for their industrial training as part of their chemistry degrees at Liverpool John Moores University.

On the journey back I felt very uncomfortable when students I played with in the school cricket and rugby teams were speculating on who would be awarded the Old Boys' Cup. This had always gone to a sixth former who had made an outstanding contribution to the school but perhaps had not made the top achievement, such as captaining the school first team. Just a few days before I had learnt that I, a fifth former, was to receive it, but I had been sworn to secrecy before it was announced and presented in the school assembly. Maybe I was chosen because I was leaving at 16 and would therefore not have the opportunity to continue my captaincy roles to the first team. As far as I am aware I am still the only person outside the sixth form to have received this accolade.

I was now suddenly faced with having to find a job, and not knowing what I wished to do.

CHAPTER 3

TIME TO GET A JOB

Having obtained only four GCEs there was no chance of me staying on in the sixth form, so in June 1958 I had to think what I would like to do and start applying for jobs. Since I had enjoyed chemistry, and it was probably my best subject, this was the first choice. In addition, at that time Teesside was probably the location of the highest concentration of the chemical industry in the UK. So I set about applying to be a Laboratory Assistant, firstly to ICI. They were the fourth or fifth largest chemical company in the world and had enormous works on both the north side of the River Tees, at Billingham, and the south side, at Wilton, near Redcar. I went for interview at Wilton, and amongst the interviewers were twins who I had watched playing for Middlesbrough rugby club. This boosted my confidence, since I thought my great rugby record at school would certainly help me to get the job. I was therefore very disappointed to find out I had been unsuccessful.

The largest and best-known steel company in the world at this time was Dorman Long, which famously provided the steel for Sydney Harbour Bridge and also for one over the river at Newcastle-on-Tyne, amongst others. On the north bank of the river Tees, near to its mouth at Port Clarence, they had a small offshoot which separated coal tar into its various chemical components. Over 350 individual chemical compounds have been detected in coal tar, although it is separated into about 10 main components by distillation, which is also the main technique used in the refining of crude oil. The coal tar was readily available from the nearby coalfields in county Durham, where it was a by-product of the conversion of coal into coke or smokeless fuel.

Ironically both these giant industrial companies have long since disappeared. Dorman Long became part of British Steel and in the early 1990s ICI split off its agrochemical and pharmaceutical divisions, plus most of its polymer interests, into a company called Zeneca. Most of this later merged with Astra Pharmaceuticals to become AstraZeneca, which is now one of the world's largest pharmaceutical companies. The agrochemicals interests became part of Syngenta.

To get to the works I had to travel through Middlesbrough and cross the river Tees on the famous Transporter bridge which carried passengers and vehicles on a moveable cradle hanging beneath the bridge. A similar bridge was built in Widnes in Cheshire across the River Mersey. Some years earlier I had enjoyed a school trip to the bridge and climbed to the very top, from where there are superb views (on a clear day). When I first started at 16 I had to catch a bus to the bridge and then walk about a mile to the works on the Durham side of the river Tees. Life got a lot easier when I passed my driving test shortly after becoming 17 and was able to buy an old Morris 8.

I started on the princely annual salary of £470 and worked from 9 until 5 from Monday to Friday. The work was interesting and varied and consisted of collecting samples and then carrying out chemical analysis to ensure that they were within specification. This applied to both the incoming coal tar and the refined products leaving the works.

At this time (1958) there were many coal mines in county Durham. Coal tar was the by-product of converting coal into coke and smokeless fuels and so was readily available and easily transported by road tanker to Port Clarence.

Not only did I have to climb on top of the road tankers to drop a sample can into the coal tar, I also had to climb on top of very large storage tanks for finished products like benzene, toluene and absorbing oil. Each tank held up to 20,000 gallons and was about 30 feet high. The sample can had a rubber stopper in the middle, which was attached to a long rope. It was lowered well below the surface of the liquid and the rope jerked to lift the stopper out and allow the liquid to fill it. On clear days there was an excellent view of the river Tees, from the Transporter Bridge past the docks to the mouth of the river, where it met the North Sea, and also of Middlesbrough.

Various tests were then carried out in the laboratory, including distillation and insoluble matter in various solvents for solid materials such as pitch, which was used in surfacing roads. The latter test involved placing a known weight of the solid in a crucible which had a porous, sintered glass layer in the middle which allowed liquid to pass through whilst retaining the solid material. Reweighing the crucible after drying enabled the weight of insoluble matter to be calculated. The procedure involved pouring boiling solvent into the crucible in the open laboratory. We were therefore exposed to the fumes on a daily basis.

Two of our solvents were of particular interest – pyridine and benzene. Pyridine was reputed to cause sterility in males, but several of my colleagues disproved this by fathering children. Benzene was to come to the fore very much later, in the 1980s, when it was shown to be carcinogenic. It is interesting and reassuring that none of us who were exposed to it regularly have, to my knowledge, had any such problems. Interestingly, very much later, around 1990, I was involved in an incident concerning benzene when I was getting my students at Liverpool Polytechnic to carry out an experiment with it. Some technicians had read that it was carcinogenic, and tried to get the Head of Department to stop us doing the experiment. When I pointed out that the reaction was being carried out in a fume cupboard and most of the benzene was consumed in the reaction, we went ahead, since nobody was exposed to the benzene. Part of the learning experience was to be able to use hazardous substances by taking the necessary precautions.

The coal tar had quite a strong smell, which I became immune to, with handling it every day. However, when I went to get my haircut the hairdresser often commented that he could detect it on my clothes.

Shortly after starting work two things happened which were to have a major influence on my life. Firstly I realised the error of my ways in not studying hard enough at school, and secondly I met Joy Pledger, who would become my wife.

CHAPTER 4

STUDY, MORE STUDY AND GETTING MARRIED

In September 1958 I started on an ONC (Ordinary National Certificate) in Chemistry course at the local technical college, Constantine College, which would eventually become Teesside University. This was a two-year day release course involving study for one day and evening, and the qualification was equivalent to a couple of A levels. Alongside it I was also taking again the GCE 'O' level (now GCSE) in English Language course which I had failed at school, but which was an essential requirement for higher level study. Unfortunately I again failed, but I managed to pass it after a resit.

At the end of my second year I successfully completed the course to gain my ONC. Even better news was to follow. On the basis of that performance the college recommended that I go on the GRIC (Graduate of the Royal Institute of Chemistry) course. This was the equivalent of a good BSc (Hons) degree and was a sandwich course which involved six months' study at college and six months' working at my company each year for four years. My employers agreed and I commenced studies in September 1960. It was a very intensive course with lectures and practical classes timetabled fully from 0900 to 1700 every day. In the evenings and at weekends we had to complete assignments and write up laboratory reports. From Monday to Friday after classes finished at 1700 I would stay and work in the college library until 2100. During my time in college I was required to go back to work during the Christmas holidays, unlike the other students, most of whom worked for ICI.

It was an excellent course, giving a good grounding across the whole range of chemistry and developing practical skills to a high level, something that employers valued highly, so they favoured these graduates over those who had followed a traditional university BSc (Hons) course. The qualification and course were administered by the Royal Institute of Chemistry and for us meant an external examination, which was made even harder because they would not publish a syllabus for the course. My fellow students had all studied for a year above me, having taken the first year of an HNC in Chemistry course, and this was to have interesting consequences when we got to the final examinations.

We were a class of about 15 students and got on well with our lecturers. I was impressed and inspired by one in particular, Dr Ted Glover. He came into the classroom and just started teaching and writing on the board with no notes to aid him. Organic chemistry was his area, and he not only made the subject very clear and interesting, but showed that with a few basic ideas a lot of the chemistry could be predicted or worked out. Although grasping these ideas was hard work for me, once I had them in my mind I could work out the chemistry of molecules which I had not previously come across. It was also a bonus if you had a poor memory. This convinced me that this was the branch of chemistry that I wished to specialise in, and it was also the area that covered coal tar chemicals.

After two years of really hard work we all passed the part I exams. In 1963 I was awarded the ICI Science Medal as the best science student – what an academic turn around! In June 1964 everyone but me sat the final part II exams. I had to wait until November because the rules required you to spend a minimum time between ONC and taking the GRIC finals. By then all my classmates had passed and gained their awards.

I sat a three-hour theory paper on the Monday morning, another on the afternoon and a third on the Tuesday morning. I then had to board a train from Middlesbrough to London and find digs for four nights. On the Wednesday morning I had to find the London School of Pharmacy, my 'home' for the next four days. On each of these days we had a six-hour practical examination. Little wonder that in the 1990s, when my own university students came to complain that they had only one day off between exams, I was not sympathetic.

In 1963 I had been moved into the Research Department and promoted from Laboratory Assistant to Research Chemist. Even better, I had received a large salary increase because I was 21. Just before Christmas 1964 I received the great news that I had passed my exams and was now entitled to put 'Grad.RIC' after my name. Although some colleagues from Dorman Long had started the course before me, I was the first to successfully complete it. My parents and my wife were immensely proud of my achievement, which takes me to that other great event of that time – getting married.

After leaving school my main sport changed from rugby to soccer. I am not sure how it came about, but I started playing for a local church youth team, St. George's Rovers. As Captain I attended the committee meetings with the officials and members of the senior team and Joy Pledger and her sister Dorothy used to serve tea in the church hall. We got chatting and I walked them home. Joy was very surprised when I asked her out – she thought I was interested in her sister!

Our first date was to Richmond, in beautiful Swaledale. From there I took her to my home, which was the Albert Cocks Memorial Home, a care home for the elderly, where my mother had been asked to become Matron when it opened in 1960. Joy was rather shocked because I had not told her that we were going to my home, and even more so a little later when this burly policeman in uniform walked in – my father!

Joy was immensely supportive and encouraging during those years of intensive studying and rarely complained, even though she hardly saw me during the week. She was working in the wages office at ICI Billingham, and one of her colleagues was to become famous and later notorious. He was Frank Bough, who was a safety officer before moving to become a sports presenter on North East television and then a national presenter on the BBC in London. Sadly he was disgraced through public announcements of his problems with drugs.

Joy and I married on the 24th August 1963 at St George's Church in Middlesbrough and after the reception we went to her parents' house in Kensington Road, right opposite Middlesbrough Football Club's Ayresome Park home. We left in my father's car, which he had loaned us for our honeymoon in Edinburgh, with cans tied on to it. This was at about 1445 on a Saturday afternoon with the Middlesbrough FC match starting at 1500, and I had to drive slowly through the groups of supporters. I stopped a short distance further on and removed all the tin cans and streamers from the car, after which we had a good journey to the B&B we had booked in Edinburgh. We did not have a very auspicious start, since I was laid low with flu for three days, but we did enjoy watching the Military Tattoo. Joy's sister Dorothy had been chief bridesmaid and a few months later Joy returned the favour when Dorothy married Morris Emmerson, a professional footballer with Middlesbrough.

Our St George's Rovers youth team won the league and then we were excited to reach the final of the cup, because it was always held on Middlesbrough's ground; what an experience to look forward to. Sadly that year it was not available and we played it on the Northern League team's South Bank ground. To add insult to injury, we got beat! Within a few years I had moved up to the senior team and a few years later on still I became Captain. We had some success winning the league and playing in a cup final, which was amazing for me. Our opponents were from a higher league and the match went to extra time. My position was right back, so I rarely scored except when I took the penalties. In extra time I badly sprained my ankle, so I hobbled to the centre forward position just to try and be a nuisance. With only a couple of minutes of extra time to go, we gained a corner. Our winger, who had played semi-professionally in his younger days, sent over a perfect ball which I headed into the net. We had won. Amazingly I had dreamed the night before that I would score the winning goal, unlikely though it was!

During this time Chris Old joined us for a season, just after he had signed for Yorkshire Cricket Club. At the end of the season they told him to give up soccer because of the risk of injury. He went on to have great success as a fast bowler, not only for 'God's Own County' of Yorkshire, but also for England. His brother Alan was also a great sportsman with caps at rugby for Yorkshire and England. My only link with Yorkshire CC was working in a snack van when they played a fixture at Middlesbrough CC.

I knew that one of my classmates from college, Tony Storey, had started a PhD at Durham University whilst I was still waiting to take my exams. He was doing well and the head of department there, Professor Ken Musgrave, had suddenly received a new research grant and was therefore looking for a research student to work on the research project. The professor contacted Ted Glover, and he in turn contacted all my group of students to see if anyone was interested. Although Joy and I barely knew what a PhD was, we decided I should apply, and after an interview I was offered the position. To accept would mean major changes to our lives, with me leaving a salaried post for a research grant, although the latter was not that much lower than the former. There was also the cost of travelling to Durham and back each day (about 40 miles), since we had just bought our first house when we married, a nice three-bedroomed semi-detached for £2, 300.

We decided it was a great opportunity, and so it was that I started my PhD in the chemistry department at Durham University in January 1965.

CHAPTER 5

CARRYING OUT RESEARCH FUNDED BY NASA

I began research studies for my Doctor of Philosophy (PhD) degree in the Chemistry Department at Durham University in January 1965. My supervisor was Professor Ken Musgrave, the Head of Department, with Dr Dick Chambers as second supervisor. Although the funding for my project, plus my maintenance grant, came from Monsanto Chemicals (one of the largest chemical companies in the world, with headquarters in the USA), it was part of a large grant to the company from NASA, the US Space Agency. This was provided for research aimed at discovering and developing new polymers which were thermally and oxidatively more stable than existing ones, and which would therefore perform better in spacecraft.

The title of my project was "The Synthesis of Highly Fluorinated Pyridines" and I spent the first month familiarising myself with the university, reading lots of published papers relating to my research and getting my laboratory equipment together. In those days there were no computers for searching the literature for research papers of interest, so it was a case of ploughing through the very large printed copies of Chemical Abstracts (CA) every few weeks, and then going to the appropriate journal for the full paper whose summary in CA looked interesting. These were weeded out from the tens of thousands of papers that were published each month. In some cases the library had to send away to the British Lending Library to obtain copies of papers in the journals which the university library did not take. Photocopiers were just coming onto the market, so we could make copies from journals.

My first task in the laboratory was to make my starting material, pentafluoropyridine, something that would take 90% of my time over the next three years. However once I had this I could carry out chemical reactions on it, nearly all of which led to entirely new compounds and so could lead to publications in research journals. The resulting new chemical compounds were then to be sent to Monsanto for testing. These were not the required polymers, but those showing up well in the tests could be used to make them.

The starting material was pyridine, a material I had been very familiar with when working in the coal tar industry. This molecule is a cyclic one consisting of five carbon atoms and one nitrogen atom linked together to form a slightly distorted hexagon. Each carbon was also joined to one hydrogen atom. My task was to replace every one of the five hydrogens with a fluorine atom. At that time this could only be done directly in very poor yield, so I had to use an indirect route. First I replaced each hydrogen with a chlorine atom, and then replaced these in turn with fluorine atoms to give pentafluoropyridine. The pyridine was reluctant to give up its hydrogens, so it had to be pushed really hard. This was done by heating the pyridine with a vast excess of a reactive chemical, called phosphorus pentachloride, in a stainless steel autoclave at 300°C for 24 hours. After cooling, the hydrogen chloride gas formed as a by-product was vented off up the fume hood. The autoclave was then opened and the excess phosphorus pentachloride destroyed by adding ice to it (with which it reacted violently). The chemical reaction between them produced more hydrogen chloride plus another chemical as gaseous products, which again vented out through the top of the fume hood.

The mixture left, after drying, consisted mainly of the required pentachloropyridine, but also products in which only four or fewer hydrogens had been replaced by chlorine, and so separation by fractional distillation was needed. The material with fewer than five chlorines in went back in the autoclave for further chlorination, as part of the next batch. The final step was to replace the five chlorines with fluorine atoms. This was done by heating the pentachloropyridine with anhydrous potassium fluoride in a Hastelloy autoclave at 480°C for 24hrs. The special alloy autoclave had to be used because of the corrosive nature of the chemicals. The product was again a mixture of the desired pentafluoropyridine, plus other materials where fewer than five chlorines had been replaced by fluorine, so again fractional distillation was used to separate them, and the more lowly fluorinated material was recycled.

As you can see, this represented almost a week's work. A bonus was that it included a body-building course! All autoclave reactions were carried out on the top floor of a separate building, which had a roof that would blow off if the pressure built up through an autoclave leaking or exploding. The first autoclave weighed about 15kgs and had to be carried across to the autoclave building and up the stairs.

Another starting material that I required was made in two steps from the pentafluoropyridine . First it was reacted in a very thick-walled sealed glass tube with ammonia gas. The second step involved using a very hazardous chemical

– hydrogen fluoride (HF). One drop on your skin will burn through to the bone in seconds. All work with it was done in a fume hood and I was provided with a visor and gauntlets made of a special polymer material. I needed an 80% aqueous solution for my reaction, so I first had to bubble anhydrous gaseous HF into water until the desired concentration was reached.

Interestingly, in 1988 I was seconded to ICI to carry out research on developing CFC replacements (see chapter 10) and before they would allow any member of staff to use HF they had to go on a week-long course!

The above illustrates some important points in chemistry, namely that very few reactions give only the desired product and therefore a great deal of time and effort has to be spent in separating and purifying them. Much research is devoted to increasing the selectivity and recycling and re-using the by-products, something that the chemical industry is very good at.

My research was in the largest area of chemistry, organic synthesis, in which over 500,000 chemists work worldwide. Their aim is to improve existing syntheses by increasing the yields or reducing the number of steps, develop new reagents, or make entirely new compounds which have desirable properties. This might be a new drug, pesticide or polymer. For the former it may be more active than an existing drug so that smaller doses are needed, or have fewer side effects, or an entirely new mode of action. Although discovering a new drug, testing it and getting it onto the market is a long and risky business (taking at least 12 years and costing over £1billion) the reward for success can be spectacular, with annual sales exceeding £1 billion in some cases.

My own interest was in making entirely new compounds, and I well remember the day I made my first. After purifying it I was really excited to look at some beautiful white crystals knowing that I was the first person on the planet ever to set eyes on them. Although I was rightly proud of my efforts, to place this in context there are more than 10 million known chemical compounds, most of them organic compounds (essentially compounds of carbon) and first made in the laboratory, with relatively few being naturally occurring compounds. The number of compounds we could make is virtually infinite, so we have so far just scratched the surface. Their influence on our lives is dealt with in chapter 15.

My research was exciting, challenging and at times frustrating, and required long hours in the lab, but it was also very rewarding. Typically, after my wife, son and I moved into a university flat I would work from nine to five, go home, have tea, and carry on in the lab from six until nine in the evening.

It was a most enjoyable three years of my life workwise

and personally, since our son Simon was born in December 1965. There were some unintended exciting times in the lab. Firstly I was carrying out a reaction in a sealed, very thick-walled, glass tube, which had heating tape around it and was being mechanically rocked. This had been placed in a fume hood in the undergraduate teaching lab next door to mine (since these students were on vacation) and had been on all night. The next morning I heard a bang and went to investigate - my foot-long glass tube was now a small pile of powdered glass!

Secondly, Don, a colleague, had left the lab at about 9pm one night and was 10 miles into his drive home when he realised that he had forgotten to turn off the heating on a still. We used this to remove water from the solvent via metallic potassium, and the vapour of the solvent was fed out, cooled back to liquid form and collected in a flask. Now potassium is a very reactive metal which reacts with air and moisture violently, often catching fire. Suddenly realising this, Don turned his Mini round and drove back at high speed (he would probably have given Lewis Hamilton a run for his money) and switched the heating off. Had he not done so the still would have boiled dry and probably exploded, spraying the highly reactive potassium around the lab.

In order to supplement my grant I spent one afternoon per week back at Constantine College, where I had studied, teaching chemistry. I found I really enjoyed it, so my mind was made up on my next career move. Even with this additional income money was always tight by the end of the month, so on the last weekend we were delighted to stay with our parents and let them feed us!

As already indicated, sport had been an important part of my life, and 1966 was a milestone. The football World Cup was held in England. In the group stage Middlesbrough's Ayresome Park hosted three matches. These all involved the virtually unknown North Korea against Italy, Russia and Chile. My wife Joy and I watched all of these and saw them defeat Italy, who went home in disgrace, whilst tiny North Korea moved onto the quarter finals against Portugal at Everton's Goodison Park, where, in a really exciting match, they eventually lost 5-3, thanks to a stellar performance by Portugal's star man, Eusebio. England would go on to defeat Portugal in the semis and Germany in the final. Interestingly the Russian team stayed and trained at Durham University.

On a personal level there were two items of interest. Firstly I joined a training session of the university team conducted by the legendary Brian Clough, who I had watched as a boy playing for Middlesbrough and England. Playing for Sunderland now, he had just damaged his knee, an injury that was to curtail his career as a player but lead to a new one as a manager, one of the best and certainly most outspoken, of all time. Secondly one of my team mates at St. George's Rovers had played semi-professional football and knew the manager of Whitby Town, who played in the same league as Bishop Auckland, a team that often won the FA Amateur Cup and provided several players for the England Amateur team. He offered to arrange a trial for me with them. However training would have involved a 70-mile round trip after a day in the lab, apart from being unfair to my wife and son, so I declined. A few years later Whitby won the FA Amateur Cup at Wembley – what if?

Although now living in Durham, I would return to Middlesbrough each Saturday to play for my soccer team. One day we were playing a works team called Head Wrightson in a cup match when after only 15 minutes I received a kick under my chin which caused it to bleed. Despite my protestations the referee insisted I went to hospital to have it stitched. This was duly done and, perhaps because I was covered in mud, the doctor decided to give me an injection of penicillin. I had previously had this applied externally on cuts.

However my face swelled and my skin became so itchy that I could not sleep. As a result I spent a week in hospital whilst they checked me out. Unfortunately I suggested to the doctors that it might have been caused by the penicillin. This suggestion by a layman probably made them put this to the back of their minds, resulting in a longer stay in hospital. So now whenever I go for any medical or dental treatment the first thing I do is to advise them of this allergy.

I was awarded my PhD in December 1967 for my thesis on pyridines. Unlike the major degree conferment event in the summer, mine was quite a small one for about 30 students receiving Masters and Doctorate Degrees. The benefit of this was that I could get lots of tickets for my family, so my wife, her parents, my parents and my great aunty were able to share the proud moment when the Vice-Chancellor awarded me my degree.

In between my meeting Joy and gaining my degree my parents had moved twice. First they moved into a brand new bungalow at Acklam on the outskirts of Middlesbrough. A few years later my maternal grandma, Amy, had been on a holiday to Cornwall and thought the mild climate was wonderful, so much so that she persuaded my parents to buy a house, and the three of them moved there. My father therefore retired from the police after 30 years of service and since he had always been a keen gardener, he bought a nursery on the Lizard Peninsula. He grew lots of Kaffir lilies and tomatoes and sold these in his shop, nicely situated on the main road from Helston to the attractive beaches of the Lizard Peninsula.

At first they lived in Gweek, several miles from the nursery. This was a nice little village, situated above the Helford River, and we were amused when Mum told us that if we bought ice creams from the only village shop we should tell them we lived locally so a cheaper price would apply! After a year or so they were able to move into a new bungalow that they had built on the nursery site. We were happy to spend our summer breaks there and although we spent some time on the beach, Joy and I enjoyed looking after the shop whilst grandma and grandad took our son Simon, and later our daughter Susan as well, to the beach, since they only saw us at Christmas and in the summer. It was a long drive from the North East (almost 350 miles) and I was the only driver at that time, so we would set off around 7 in the evening with Simon lying on the back seat and sleeping most of the way until we arrived about 10 the next morning. I could just still keep awake! In those days the M5 was only partly completed, so we had to leave it at Bristol, cross the Avonmouth Bridge and rejoin the motorway, which only went as far as Taunton. This still left almost 100 miles to go.

CHAPTER 6

STARTING AN ACADEMIC CAREER

At the end of my PhD I was offered a temporary lectureship at Salford University for one year, covering for a lecturer who was spending a year at a Canadian University. The first three months were difficult since I not only had lectures to prepare, and research to carry out, but Joy and Simon had to stay with her parents in Middlesbrough until we bought a house. My aunty and uncle lived in a village near Chester and let me stay with them during the week. This meant a 70-mile round trip each day and then on Friday afternoon I would drive the 120-plus miles back to Middlesbrough, returning early Monday morning – all this in a rather old Mark 1 Ford Cortina.

For the rest of that year life was much easier after we moved into our house in Whitefield near Bury, just a 15-minute drive from the university. At the time Joy was pregnant with our second child, and Susan was born at home on the 19th February1969, amidst great excitement because she was the first girl in the Heaton family for several generations. Some months later the car had to be scrapped and we remained without one for several months until we could afford one. As a result our trips to Cornwall were made by train from Manchester and we still vividly remember the one at Christmas 1968. We had two young children, two cases (one full of clothes and one of Christmas presents for our children) and were travelling just before Christmas. A change at Plymouth was necessary and when our new train arrived from London it was so packed that we spent the next hour sitting on the cases in the luggage van! We were delighted that my mum was able to travel back with us, and our additional luggage was three large boxes of gladioli, which my parents had grown at their nursery, and which we would sell to our local shop.

Life personally and professionally was enjoyable but challenging, particularly my teaching, because my research area of organofluorine chemistry is outside, and rather different from, the mainstream organic chemistry that I was teaching. Not only had I to write my lectures but I had to re-learn some of the material; tutorials were a particular challenge, with students able to ask any questions they liked.

Our young family was thriving, with Simon starting school and Susan sleeping most of the time. Visits to Joy's family in the North East were also made by train and she did well to cope on her own with getting two young children and a large Silver Cross pram on to the train, and then changing to the local train for Middlesbrough at Darlington.

At that time the Chemistry Department at Salford University was the largest in the UK, with over 60 academic staff. As well as running BSc and post-graduate courses and research, they also offered the Grad.RIC course which I had taken at Constantine College. The difference here was that it was an internal course with the university staff setting the exams. The finals still included six-hour practical exams and at the end of the last one the Head of Department, Professor Ramage, got his secretaries to go and purchase an ice cream for each of the 60 students, which they received and ate in the laboratory. Where was health and safety then?

Since it became clear that I would not be offered a permanent position at Salford University I had to start looking for a job towards the end of 1968. I had an open mind, but I really enjoyed teaching and after unsuccessful interviews at Beecham's Pharmaceuticals (later to become part of GSK) and Monsanto Chemicals at Ruabon in North Wales, I was offered a lectureship at Liverpool Regional

College of Technology, with a start date of January 1st 1969. I telephoned them to point out that I would not actually start on New Year's Day but on the 2nd of January! Joining the college meant that I was employed by Liverpool City Council, which was to make life interesting some years later. The move also meant a significant increase in salary of around £400 per annum, to over £1, 800.

Just as when I had started at Salford University, for the first three months travel became a significant factor. Following the demise of our Cortina I had to travel to Liverpool by train each day. This meant a 10-minute walk to our local Besses o' the Barn station, a 20-minute journey to Manchester Victoria, and then a change of train for the 50-minute journey to Liverpool Lime Street. The college was then only 10 minutes' walk away, but sometimes I had a 9 am class at some labs which had been owned by Tate and Lyle, the sugar refiners. They were located near the docks and a 25-minute walk from the station. All of this necessitated my leaving home by 6 am and rarely getting home in the evening before seven. As a result I only saw my baby daughter awake at the weekends.

Clearly finding and buying a house in the Liverpool area was our first priority, and second was buying a car. Most of my new colleagues lived either in the Formby/Southport area or on the Wirral, which is that area of land across the River Mersey from Liverpool and with the River Dee as its western boundary. My new line manager, Dr Peter Jones, lived in Formby, and he kindly collected us from the station one weekend and took us around that area looking at houses. At that time my only knowledge of the Wirral was of the industry on the Merseyside of the peninsula, so when we hired a car for our first look around we were very surprised to see some very nice rural areas with much greenery. We soon chose a three-bedroom detached house in Bromborough and agreed to purchase it. This was at the time when the monopoly of solicitors for house conveyancing had been challenged and broken. Unfortunately the seller chose an organisation that was feeling its way in dealing with this legal side. They were extremely slow, and before the deal was completed the seller started a new job in Bristol but decided he did not like it, so he cancelled the sale. Even worse, house prices had started to take off and we could no longer afford that sort of house in that area. We therefore started looking again on the Dee side of the Wirral in Neston, which proved a blessing in disguise, because we were able to purchase a four-bedroom detached for the same sort of price. On the downside the public transport links to Liverpool were nothing like as good and in 1969 the train was the only option. Neston station was a 20-minute walk from our house with trains to Liverpool running only every hour, taking that long to get there, and involving a change of train at Bidston.

As at Salford, my appointment was as a Lecturer in Organic Chemistry but the difference was that here the priority was very much on teaching, with research being something that people did on top. At universities the emphasis was the other way round with careers depending on published research rather than teaching performance. Since teaching was what I enjoyed most, the new position was ideal.

Like Salford, Liverpool Regional College of Technology Chemistry Department also offered a BSc (Hons) degree in Chemistry and an internal Grad.RIC course. In addition to teaching Organic Chemistry and administrative duties I was also charged with developing a new course – a BSc (Hons) in Industrial Chemistry, which would be almost unique. Funding had already been agreed for a large new semi-technical Industrial Chemistry lab, widely found in the chemical industry but only in Chemical Engineering departments in academia. In ordinary chemistry labs, reactions are typically carried out in glass flasks of 100-250 millilitre (mls) size and occasionally up to 2 litres (2,000 mls). Our new lab would be equipped with flasks of 100 litres, with distillation columns 10 metres in height attached to them, plus other similar-sized units.

All this was well beyond my experience, so we took advice from local industrialists and worked closely with the company supplying the equipment (James Jobling from

Stone in Staffordshire) in designing and equipping the lab. We also worked with specialists in supplying equipment for high-pressure reactions (Thomas Cook from Birmingham) to equip an autoclave bay. No problem here since, as described in Chapter 5, I was using autoclaves almost daily at Durham University.

In order to gain experience I spent several weeks during the summer of 1970 seconded to Zeneca's manufacturing site in Macclesfield. This is now part of AstraZeneca, one of the largest pharmaceutical companies in the world. I was working in the area where they make larger quantities of potential new drugs (10-20 kgs) for further testing after promising initial results. I gained experience in carrying out reactions in 50-litre vessels, where care and continuous monitoring were needed, since some were performed in flammable solvents like ether, and some reactions were exothermic (generating heat). If the reaction became too vigorous it could 'runaway' with potentially disastrous results.

Over the next 15 years we successfully launched the degree in Industrial Chemistry, as a four-year sandwich course like the existing chemistry degree, where each student was placed in industry for the whole of the third year. This style of course was the province of the Colleges of Technology, many of which later became Polytechnics (in 1970), and were renowned for their excellent teaching. The value of that year's experience is now appreciated, with practically all universities offering the placement as part of the degree course, or just work experience.

We started by assessing the year with the industrial supervisor during the two visits by a college tutor and counted the marks towards the students' degree. Later we separated it off and awarded a 'Certificate of Professional Development' for successful completion of this year. In addition to applying the chemistry they had learned in college, the students gained experience of new chemical techniques. They also matured, and could decide, on a rational basis, if they wanted to work in industry when they finished their degree.

In the latter respect one young lady stands out in my mind. I visited her at a company called International Paints, which made specialist paints for marine applications. Her project involved speeding up the analysis of the batches of paint so that they could be released for canning more quickly. This involved lots of interaction with the workers on the plant as she regularly went to collect samples. As a result she decided she wanted a career that was more people oriented, and therefore joined Marks & Spencers Graduate Recruitment Scheme.

For many years I had the major administrative role of Industrial Training Tutor with the job of placing all the students with industrial companies, assigning colleagues as visiting tutors and processing all the results at the end of the year. As well as visiting several students myself I spent a lot of time visiting companies in order to arrange placements. With my previous experience in the chemical industry I was a natural fit and I thoroughly enjoyed the role. The downside was that all this was done on top of my normal teaching load.

During these years I was promoted to Senior Lecturer in Organic Chemistry (1975) and then Reader in Industrial Chemistry (1983). During the early part of this period there were severe funding problems for Liverpool City Council (led by Derek Hatton) and confrontation with the government, which led to us all receiving our redundancy notices. As a result I made my first-ever appointment with my bank manager, which necessitated a trip to Salford, in order to make contingency plans in case the worst happened. Fortunately it never came to that, but one of my new colleagues set something of a record by being appointed and receiving his redundancy notice all within a few days!

In 1992 the Liverpool Polytechnic became Liverpool John Moores University (LJMU), named after the head of the family which had made its fortune running Littlewoods football pools and stores. As a result we were no longer employed by Liverpool City Council but by the university.

We had settled well in our home in Neston and become involved in the local community. Our children were at

Neston Primary School and my wife served on the Parent Teachers' Association committee. Simon played for the school soccer team and Susan for the gymnastics and athletics teams so, like many parents, we became supporters and taxi drivers!

In 1973 I was up a ladder painting the outside of my house when from next door, I heard a voice say "just carry on painting across here"! This was my introduction to the family who were moving in next door. With them and another family we became founder members of Neston Swimming Club, and we have all stayed firm friends ever since, although our neighbour sadly passed away in 2005. He introduced us to golf and crown green bowls, and the other friend and I continued to play golf together until ill health prevented him in 2015. However we both continue to play competitive bowls having started at Neston (both of us serving as Chairman) before he moved house, and joined his local team, Royden Hall. In 2009 I joined Heswall RBL bowling club and still play for them.

In the early 1970s I joined two institutions which were to play a major role in my life. In 1971, in its second year of operation, I became a Tutor/Counsellor for the Open University for its Science Foundation Course, S100. This brought in much-needed additional income, since we had agreed that my wife would not get a job again until the children were near to leaving school. This is discussed further in Chapter 8.

One of my colleagues, Dr Alex Wood, was the Hon. Secretary of the Liverpool Section of the multidisciplinary, international, Society of Chemical Industry (SCI), and in December 1973 he persuaded me to join. This would give me opportunities to meet industrialists who could be helpful with our Industrial Chemistry course and industrial placements for my students. I have been active in the society ever since and I am currently an elected member of its Board of Trustees and chair its Early Career Committee. More details are given in the following chapters.

I had joined the Royal Institute of Chemistry as a student member in order to study for my Grad.RIC and have remained a member ever since, serving on local, regional and national/international committees from 1990 onwards. Details are given later in this book.

CHAPTER 7

PROMOTING CHEMISTRY TO YOUNG PEOPLE, AND TEACHING IN MALAYSIA

In the late 1980s and early 1990s the popularity of chemistry had declined, so attracting enough students to keep our courses going was an uphill struggle. As a 'soft sell' to publicise our department and courses, we offered popular science talks/demonstrations to sixth formers in their schools, and I toured the country giving a presentation entitled "Pesticides, Bane or Boon?" over 50 times. Most interestingly I was also invited to give a talk at a chemistry careers meeting for school teachers, organised by the Royal Society of Chemistry, at Salter's Hall in London. This was on a Saturday and all the teachers wore casual clothes except one, who wore a suit and dicky bow. During lunch he asked me if I would be prepared to give a talk to his school science society when I was down in London. Having agreed, I was rather taken aback when he said his school was Eton!

We later finalised a date, I gave my presentation on "Pesticides Bane or Boon" and then I was given overnight accommodation in a Housemaster's quarters in the largest bedroom I have ever seen – bigger than the lounge in my house. I had to leave shortly after 8 am the next morning to catch a train back to Liverpool in order to lecture in the afternoon. The housemaster was in his formal dress of tails and apologised because his housekeeper was not yet on duty. He managed to make me some toast, after admitting he had never used the toaster before! As the taxi taking me to Slough Station passed through the school grounds I was amused to see that many of the pupils (dressed in their formal attire) had newspapers under their arms, but almost as many had *The Sun* as *The Times*! I was very flattered to be told that the previous speaker to the Science Society had been Lord Krebs, the prominent zoologist, who is now President of the British Science Association.

In 1983, with the support of the committee of SCI Liverpool Section (of which I was now a member) I started the LJMU/SCI Schools/Industry project – I was to run it for the next 20 years. Its aim was to give schoolchildren a better understanding and awareness of the chemical industry and its contribution to our lives. We did this by bringing in young people who worked in the industry to give short lectures/demonstrations. I would start things off with demonstrations to the whole group, with the help of a few pupils, including "turning water into wine" and "making polymers". The project was immensely successful with over 12,000 pupils and teachers attending the meetings at LJMU. For me it was immensely enjoyable but an additional claim on my time, since I not only organised the meetings but had to raise sponsorship from industry.

Another outreach activity that I ran each year, initially with Salters Livery Company and later the Royal Society of Chemistry, was a Festival of Chemistry. This involved secondary schools sending teams of four to the university to carry out chemical tests in order to solve a mystery, and also see a lecture/demonstration, whilst the judges decided on the first three teams who received prizes, and every participant received a memento of the occasion. On one occasion I was delighted to be able to get Claire Sweeney, a star of the TV soap *Brookside*, to present the prizes. We had great fun with the pupils beforehand when I told them that the prizes would be presented by someone from Brookside. Most of them guessed that it would be Jimmy Corkhill – something Claire enjoyed teasing them about! It was always a most enjoyable day for everyone, and something I carried on doing each year from 1990 until my early retirement in

2005. One of my colleagues, Dr Ian Bradshaw, took it over and has expanded it. These events achieved their purpose of interesting the pupils in Chemistry and showing that it could be exciting and enjoyable. It also enabled them to experience the university environment and persuade some of them to go on and study Chemistry at university, with a few of them coming to LJMU.

I pursued these activities because I felt chemistry had been good to me so I wanted to "put something back" and enthuse young people to enjoy the subject as I had, and also because I enjoyed doing them. I have been very lucky throughout my professional career in doing things that I really enjoyed so that I looked forward to going to work each day. Indeed I still continue to promote chemistry to young people even today, as Chair of the SCI's Early Career Committee, although now with older people, since these are university students.

However in 2010/2011 I managed a project at the other end of the age scale – primary school children. At the time I served on the RSC's North West Trust, a wonderful committee, because all we did was to provide funding for worthwhile educational projects, usually related to the chemical industry. It was set up with funds from the RSC Manchester Section, which, for many years, had run a very successful and profitable Labex exhibition and then sold it. Here companies would pay for a stand to display and sell their laboratory equipment.

For many years I had also been a Trustee at Catalyst Science Discovery Centre in Widnes. The trust provided some funding each year for activities such as Christmas lectures at Catalyst, but we decided to be proactive rather than reactive by undertaking a major project with them. After discussion with their Education Officer, Sue Halliday, we agreed to produce a DVD on Primary Science Practical Work to help teachers. Since few of these teachers had much formal scientific training, it would show them how exciting, spectacular, practical science could be done in everyday household equipment like measuring jugs, and using everyday products obtainable from supermarkets as the 'chemicals'. The teachers could practise the experiments at home by following the DVD and become confident before doing them in school with the children. The worries about the dangers and health and safety which the general public has when 'chemicals' are mentioned are overcome by using everyday products which can be bought at the supermarket.

Sue and a collaborator, Lorelly Wilson, would be filmed by a professional media company, carrying out, and giving a commentary on, the experiments at Catalyst. The budget was £15,000 and we twice approached the Royal Society of Chemistry for funding, but were turned down each time without any valid reasons being given. However the NW Trust Committee were so enthused with the project that they agreed to provide all the funding. The DVD was immensely successful, with over 10,000 copies being distributed to teachers in the UK, Eire and South Africa. Ironically some years ago all its content was put on the RSC website as supporting material for teachers and can be accessed at www.rsc.org, then Learn Chemistry, where it has been split into several shorter videos.

In the late 1990s the Polytechnics in the north of England formed the Northern Consortium and this developed links with the Institute Technology Mara in Shah Alam near Kuala Lumpur in Malaysia. As a result UK staff went out there for short periods to help with the teaching, and the students spent the final year of their BSc courses at one of our Polytechnics. The courses were mainly in sciences and engineering but also included law. In 1999 I was seconded to the college for seven weeks to teach Organic Chemistry. Before this the lady who I would liaise and teach with came to England to visit the Polytechnics for a few weeks and spent a day with me, studying our practical classes. At her request I provided her with copies of our experimental sheets.

We got off to the worst possible start on arrival in Kuala Lumpur. My wife and I were met at the airport by our driver, who spoke virtually no English, and we had no details of where we would be living. He drove around Shah Alam for some time, knocking on a few doors without reply.

I was just about to tell him to take us to a hotel for the night when a door was answered, and this was our new home. It was a house only 10 minutes' walk from the college and which we would share with other UK staff. Although the bedrooms were air-conditioned the large lounge and kitchen were not and so the patio doors were left wide open. We were horrified one night when a cockroach the size of my hand flew in, but we quickly managed to kill it once it had landed on the floor. For a while we also had great fun when every time we switched on the kitchen light a large cockroach would scurry back under the fridge! The housing complex was actually owned by the Sultan of Brunei.

After my heavy teaching and administrative duties at home, my time in Malaysia was more like a holiday, with only 12 hours' teaching per week and no other duties, so I took the opportunity to rewrite my lecture notes and prepare lots of handouts for my students. Health and safety rules in the lab were somewhat primitive compared with the UK and I was amazed in the first lab class not only to recognise the experiment, but also to see the Liverpool Polytechnic heading at the top – they had not even bothered to substitute their own institution there! I was also surprised that despite having so little to do, I was the first to arrive and the last to leave each day.

We were very honoured when my Malaysian colleague invited us, plus a lecturer from Sheffield Polytechnic and his wife, to her home for dinner and to meet her family. They were devout Muslims and when we arrived we had to wait for her husband to come down as he was still praying. His wife served us lots of nice food but would not sit down with us, saying she would dine later. However she and her two children did join us for dinner at a local restaurant the following week.

Not only did I have a light teaching load, I only had a lecture first thing on a Friday and no teaching on a Monday. The very long weekends gave us an ideal opportunity to explore the country in our hire car. It was a delight to revisit some places and also tour some new ones. We went back to Singapore, where we had spent a week in 1988 after two weeks in the Maldives in order to celebrate our silver wedding anniversary, and to Kuantan in the East of Malaysia, where we had spent a holiday some years earlier. A bonus when booking accommodation was to mention where I was working (essentially for the Malaysian government), which immediately got us a 25% discount. In Kuantan this enabled us to stay at the very upmarket Tanjong Jara hotel, particularly noted for the large number of turtles that came ashore on their beach to lay their eggs. Unfortunately we were there at the wrong time of the year and missed this.

We went on a memorable, organised trip to Lake Chini. After being bussed into the jungle, two Germans and my wife and I were seated singly behind each other in what looked like a dugout tree trunk, although it did have an outboard motor at the rear. So small was the stream that we were travelling up initially that the motor had to be frequently lifted out of the water. As we moved into a proper river the guide pointed out a King Cobra on the opposite river bank and manoeuvred the boat towards it, asking if we would like to go closer. Now snakes are my biggest dread in life, so I was very relieved when one of the Germans did not want to go any closer!

Shortly afterwards we emerged from the river to see a magnificent view – the large expanse of Lake Chini and its thousands of water lilies. We were then taken ashore to a village to meet members of the Orang Asli (the original inhabitants of Malaysia), who demonstrated their expertise with their enormous blowpipes – over six feet long.

Our most memorable new trip was to the Cameron Highlands. This is an area some 120 miles north of Kuala Lumpur, over 3,000 feet high. As a result it is cooler than the rest of the country and wealthy Malaysians like to retreat to there in the hot summer months. It is also the tea-growing area of Malaysia. The spectacular road winds through the forest, gradually ascending through the trees over several miles.

We had an interesting encounter in the hotel we stayed in. After dinner we retired into the lounge and got chatting to an English couple. Of course it was not long before the conversation got round to "where do you come from?" We said that we came from the Wirral, and they said they knew where it was and asked where on it we lived. We told them we lived in Little Neston, a little village they had probably never heard of. Not only had they heard of it, but they lived in the next village – Burton – and were on a golfing holiday!

Even this amazing coincidence pales when compared to that of our son Simon and his girlfriend Sarah (later to become his wife) when they were backpacking around the world. They were walking along a deserted beach in Fiji when they saw a lone figure approaching. As the figure drew near it turned out to be a girl Sarah had gone to school with. Surely the odds against this must have been tens of millions to one.

Our new experiences also included Malacca, a fascinating Dutch-influenced town south of Kuala Lumpur. I still have two drawings of views there, framed and hung on the walls of my study; purchased for 50p each and framed locally for a few pounds.

We also enjoyed a long weekend on the island of Pangkor, parking our car on the mainland before boarding the ferry and checking into our hotel on the beach.

One of my Biology colleagues took us on a walk round a coastal park where we were delighted to see silver-backed monkeys climbing in the trees. Another treat on the way home was stopping at a restaurant by a river and seeing hundreds of fireflies lighting up the dark.

We also saw the main tourist sites in Kuala Lumpur, and ascended the famous Petronas twin towers. A particular favourite was Chinatown, where I enjoyed learning to haggle, with an experienced colleague advising that you should never end up paying more than half the initial price quoted! We found "Rolex" watches available for the equivalent of £10! When a colleague bought one the stall holder insisted on being photographed with him, something that would come back to haunt the stall holder. He kept saying there was a money-back guarantee with the watch, knowing that tourists were unlikely ever to return. However, back in England the watch stopped after about six months. Another colleague was going to Malaysia to teach, so he was persuaded to take the watch plus the photo back to the stall. No doubt the stallholder was shocked, but he did provide a replacement watch.

Our flight home was the only time we have ever been over the luggage weight limit, mainly because we had bought several wooden carvings plus several wooden salad bowl sets for our family. The Malaysian Airlines lady realised we had been working for the government and let us through without any excess baggage charge.

CHAPTER 8

TUTORING FOR THE OPEN UNIVERSITY

The Open University (OU) was the brainchild of Jennie Lee, a member of the Labour Government of Harold Wilson, who strongly supported the idea and helped bring it to fruition in 1970. It was nicknamed the "University of the Air" and was probably the largest distance learning project in Europe, if not in the world. Its headquarters were, and remain, at Walton Hall in Milton Keynes, one of England's 'new towns', built in the 1960s to cater for the rapidly growing population of cities like London. The campus houses not only a large group of administrative, support and academic staff but also laboratories and TV studios for filming the TV programmes, which are an important part of the courses.

In 1971 I was appointed as a Tutor/Counsellor (T/C) for the Science Foundation Course (S100) at the start of the university's second year of operation. Note that the OU year runs from January to October/November, in contrast to the usual academic year from October to June. I was one of two S100 Tutor/Counsellors based at Birkenhead Technical College study centre, where the OU hired facilities for evening tutorials. The courses were unique in the UK as the only university ones that did not require the student to have any prior qualifications for entrance. They consisted of course booklets and assignments, supporting TV broadcasts, tutorials in local study centres (although for some higher-level courses people in rural areas, eg Devon, might have to travel 50 miles each way on a Saturday), and, in some cases, residential components. The latter could range from a couple of weekends to a full week in the summer at an established university, where the OU hired the facilities whilst the host's undergraduate students were on vacation. In addition S100 students received a gigantic kit of apparatus for carrying out home experiments, and it arrived just before Christmas – what a present!

The Science Foundation Course covered four areas of science, namely Biology, Chemistry, Earth Science and Physics, and the T/C was required to teach two of these areas, with specialist tutors covering the other two. I obviously covered Chemistry and also Physics (as far as I was concerned the lesser of the other three 'evils' and an area I had previously studied, unlike Biology and Earth Science). For our students taking higher level courses we had only a counselling role. In addition to the formal contact we were also available on the telephone at any time. I was fortunate that in my 25-plus years my students rang me only at sensible times. However some colleagues had tales of sometimes being woken at midnight!

Compared with my full-time university teaching job the OU was very challenging in several respects. Bear in mind that conventional university students all have pretty much the same 'A' level passes, although slightly varying grades, and are nearly all aged 18-22, so I was teaching a uniform cohort. At this time the OU students were paying their own fees and almost all were working full time with a few (mainly married) women in part-time employment. Being mature students, most had their own homes and a family to support. Their previous education and experience varied widely. Over my career they ranged from an 18-year-old who had failed his GCSEs to a married woman with four children and a 78-year-old woman who was a former teacher and had a PhD.

Giving a tutorial to a group with such a varied academic base and making it interesting and useful to all was exceedingly challenging. Another difference from my fulltime students was that the OU ones asked lots of questions and were not afraid to challenge my answers, which was great. The result was that I had to think much more about my subject and how to present it. This undoubtedly helped me to improve my teaching ability. We also marked the set assignments for our students, although the marking was monitored by a member of the course team in Milton Keynes. However the exam at the end of the course was marked by the course team and, as in conventional universities, moderated by an External Examiner from another university.

Most university staff felt that OU staff had an easy ride, with much less onerous administrative duties, no daily teaching, little research, and increasingly over the years, little student counselling. However they had to come up with innovative teaching materials and methods, bearing in mind their 'clientele'. Having lots of thinking time clearly helped and their course material and TV programmes were absolutely top class. All of us part-time staff were able to use some of this with our own students.

In the first few years the one area where I lacked experience was in the Summer Schools. When a second Science Staff Tutor, Dr Michael Gagan, was appointed to our Manchester Regional Office I drew his attention to this, and the following year I was appointed to the S100 Summer

School at Stirling University. Around 200 students participated at these each week and the teaching team consisted of a Course Director (usually a full-time employee from Milton Keynes or a Regional Staff Tutor like Mike) and about 20 tutors, five for each of the four scientific disciplines. In each team one acted as the Senior Tutor and was responsible for organising the laboratory and tutorial teaching for their area.

The Course Director (CD) held a briefing meeting for all tutors on the Saturday morning and in the afternoon we all attended the CD's welcome and briefing meeting for the students. After dinner there was a session in the lecture theatre for all students, where the Earth Science tutors provided information about the field study trip that they would be going on on Sunday morning, and the Chemistry tutors carried out a demonstration relating to one of their laboratory experiments. Some years later, as Senior Tutor, I was carrying out the demonstration. It was to illustrate the differing amounts of light absorbed by chemical species and how we would later use this to measure the concentration of species in a mixture. Part of the demonstration involved putting coloured filters (red, blue, etc) in turn into the light beam and explaining the effects of these. One of my tutors had volunteered to do this whilst I explained what was happening. However, unusually, the results did not seem to fit with my explanations, leaving me very perplexed; not a very good start to the week with an audience of 200 students, for something that had been run hundreds of times without any problems. It was only later that my colleague sheepishly confessed to me that he was colour blind!

Starting Sunday afternoon, each student would spend three half-day sessions, each of three and a half hours, in the laboratory on each of three areas of the course, carrying out experiments. There was not enough time to do this in the fourth area, so they were given a quick run through this on Friday afternoon before the final debriefing session for everyone and the end of the school. Everyone had Wednesday afternoon and evening free in order to recharge their batteries. Evening tutorials were offered from 7-8 pm and 8-9 pm, with a choice from each of the four disciplines on Sunday, Monday, Tuesday and Thursday evenings. There was always a very good attendance at these, even though they were optional.

Students received a satisfactory certificate of attendance provided that they had attended most sessions and made a reasonable effort in the laboratory. This was needed to pass the course, unless excusal from the Summer School had been granted.

At most campuses there were several OU courses running simultaneously, which resulted in up to 1,000 students being present most weeks, and the OU Students'

Association organised social activities such as discos and quizzes.

The way that virtually all students helped and supported each other, both in the groups at the local study centre and at the Summer Schools, was immensely satisfying. This, plus enjoying the social events at the latter, made for a tremendous camaraderie amongst virtually the whole group of students and tutors at the school. This definitely helped everyone not only to enjoy the week but to learn a lot and make tremendous progress in a very short time. I was amazed to see people who had hardly ever been in a laboratory confidently carrying out experiments by the end of the third session. When I later moved to teaching at the second level Chemistry Summer School (CHEM999) the progress and range of techniques used during the week were even more remarkable. Some students also loved meeting the TV stars from Walton Hall who had appeared on the course TV programmes. In fact one female chemistry star received marriage proposals!

One year whilst I was at the second level school at Nottingham University (its only location) I was chatting on the phone to my wife when she drew my attention to an article in the *News of the World*. One of its reporters had been travelling on a train and got chatting to a couple of young women who were on their way to Summer School, and they had disclosed that they had removed their wedding rings. The rather sensational article then implied that there were lots of relationships going on at the schools. It is not surprising that in such an environment, with lots of social activities, and most people having a few drinks (or more!) in the evening, some liaisons will develop. However from my view it was a very small proportion of the student body and to imply it was more (which of course the article did) ignored the incredibly hard work of nearly all the students, who were amazingly highly motivated to learn as much as possible during the week.

I spent over 20 years teaching for one or two weeks each year at the Summer Schools, for the first five or so on the S100 course at Reading or Stirling universities, and then the CHEM999 second level course at Nottingham University. On a number of occasions I was appointed Senior Tutor and twice Course Director. Most weeks I shared with several colleagues who I had previously worked with, which made the week even more enjoyable. It was also instructive to see how they had tackled things I had done, such as debriefing experiments.

What was also interesting was finding out what the students did for a living. One year at Reading I was incapacitated, having received a nasty bite from a horsefly whilst walking from our accommodation to the labs, which caused my leg to really swell and the tissues to harden. At the university medical centre I was given antibiotics, and for the next two days my colleagues put me in a wheelchair and wheeled me across the campus to the laboratory. There I sat at the front in the chair while my students came up to me with their queries. Sadly I could not participate in the Thursday evening disco, but I did attend in my wheelchair, and got chatting to an older student. He had been in my group in the lab and I had noticed how slow, but methodical and precise, he had been in doing the experiments. When I asked him what he did for a living I was surprised to learn that he was a surgeon; perhaps this was less surprising so in the light of the way he worked in the lab. He was taking the course to update and improve his knowledge of science.

On one of the weeks when I was Course Director the week ran smoothly and enjoyably until the Thursday evening. We had enjoyed the weekly disco and a group of the tutors and students were enjoying chatting and having final drinks back at our accommodation, when one of the students became agitated. He disclosed that he had been suffering from depression and the music at the disco had brought back sad memories of his divorce. We tried to calm him down, but he rushed off. It was probably around 1 am. Being concerned for his welfare, some of the other tutors and I started searching for him. He was not in his room, nor had the security staff at the gates seen anyone leaving the campus. Now Nottingham University has a large open campus, so there was not much more that we could do.

However, unknown to us, the security staff had phoned the police and they duly arrived. They wanted to check the student's room but the porter's key would not work, so a ladder was obtained and they climbed up it to the open window, but could see no sign of anyone.

At that point the student wandered up to us and apologised. The police asked me if one of us would stay outside his room for the rest of the night, but I vetoed this, pointing out that it was now 4 am and we all had to have had breakfast and be ready to teach in the labs at 9 am. The student came to see me the next morning and apologise and thank us. However I still had to write and submit a full report on the incident.

We all looked forward each year to receiving our letter of appointment. What could be better than enjoying teaching such highly-motivated students, having a great time socially and being reasonably well-paid with all food and accommodation provided? In return we did work very long hours.

As indicated previously, quite a number of my colleagues became close friends, some continuing even today, though some, sadly, have passed away.

My OU teaching in the 1970s provided much needed additional income, for although I earned a decent salary at my university, bringing up two young children, buying a house and running a car was a financial challenge for my wife and me. As previously indicated, we had agreed that she would not return to work until the children had left school, so we relied on my income alone. Professionally it was the busiest time of my life. At Liverpool Poly I had a full teaching load, was setting up a new Industrial Chemistry Laboratory and also undertaking key administrative roles. Although the OU was part time, at times, such as marking assignments (which had to be turned around quite quickly and feedback given), plus weekly tutorials, it seemed almost like a full-time job. On top of all this I was writing my first textbook in the evenings and at weekends.

Summing up my long experience as an OU tutor, it was hard work and challenging, but immensely rewarding to teach such highly-motivated students and see their amazing achievements. The challenge was in teaching disparate groups, whose academic abilities and experiences varied so much. Their questions and challenges to some of my answers made me think more deeply about my subject and also encouraged me to devise better ways of presenting it. Some of my proudest memories were of seeing students who had started out with no academic qualifications going on to gain their degrees, and good ones at that. Amongst the hundreds of students that I taught was a married woman who had four children, a house to run with her husband and a part-time job, and she gained a first-class honours degree.

How impressive is that? It also confirms that in many respects the OU was the university of the second chance, because most of my students clearly could have gained a degree if they had followed the conventional route via 'A' levels, but had not done so for personal reasons.

In the latter part of my OU career I also acted as a consultant to the university, checking and proof-reading assignments and also writing two industrial chemistry case studies for the course books for the S205 course entitled 'The Molecular World'.

As I have indicated previously, the experience definitely helped me to become a better teacher and helped me always to get excellent feedback on my performance from students and during university inspections and reviews.

CHAPTER 9

BECOMING A PUBLISHED AUTHOR

My first sortie into writing textbooks was in 1976, when I and my three colleagues who also taught Organic Chemistry at Liverpool Polytechnic decided to help our students by writing a short paperback entitled "Elementary Organic Qualitative Analysis". We paid for the printing of this and sold copies to our students, who would use it extensively as part of their laboratory work. Eventually we managed to cover our costs and make a small profit – hardly much of a reward for the hours that we had spent producing the booklet. In 1981 we published a second edition.

My venture into commercial publishing started in 1982 with an unexpected visit from Dr Keith Whittles. He had been visiting someone else and had been flipping through some information on the poly when he came across my details. He was a commissioning editor for Blackies, a publisher based in Glasgow. Although a qualified geologist, he had identified a gap in the undergraduate market for a textbook on Industrial Chemistry. He enquired if I would be interested in writing this or if not in recommending someone who might be. I agreed to be the author and he appreciated at the outset that it was a very broad topic, which was probably the main reason why there was no suitable book on the market. Since no individual would have such broad expertise, we agreed that it would need a team of authors. I would write some of the chapters and act as editor, and we would bring on board experts for each of the remaining chapters. Clearly this would complicate production immensely and getting everyone to deliver on time would be a big challenge. Not only that, but they would be a mixture of academics and people working in industry. Personal experience had already shown me that some academics are not very good at meeting deadlines, eg submitting exam questions on time. Keith had already identified a few people whom we could approach.

Since the book would be in a niche area or market, rather than mainstream, I was keen for us to first establish some idea of the potential market and sales. I therefore proposed carrying out a survey by writing to every UK university and college chemistry and chemical engineering department and asking them for details of the modules and courses which they ran in the area of industrial chemistry. This would not only help to inform the decision on whether or not to go ahead with the book, but if we decided against I could at least publish the results of the survey. Of course we did agree to proceed, and I also published the results in the Royal Society of Chemistry's journal, Chemistry in Britain, (Chem.Br. 1982, 18 (3), 162).

Once we had decided to go ahead, the first step was to recruit the team of authors ready for the challenging times ahead. Even producing my own chapters (approximately 25% of the book) on time created a lot of pressure, because I had a full teaching load plus a major administrative task as Professional Training Tutor on top. The latter involved placing all our students in industry for the third year of their four-year sandwich course, organising colleagues to visit each of them at least twice, assess them in conjunction with the industrial supervisor, and finally collate all the marks and submit them to the exam board. As already explained I also had a part-time (it often felt more like full-time) job as Tutor-Counsellor for the Open University. In addition I had started the SCI/LJMU Schools Industry project, for which I not only organised the meetings but had to go out to industry to raise the funding to support it. At this time our children were teenagers and like many parents my wife and I were busy 'taxi drivers', taking them to various events and activities. No pressure there then!

Having 'burned the midnight oil' for several months both writing and editing the book, the manuscript was delivered to Keith, at Blackies, ahead of the deadline. Following proof reading of the entire book, and compiling the index, it was very exciting several months later to receive a copy of the cover, and in 1984 *An Introduction to Industrial Chemistry* was duly published. Joy, who had typed my contributions, and my parents and family shared my excitement, pride and satisfaction at this landmark.

The royalties would certainly not make me rich, and in terms of the hours spent writing the book represented a poor rate of pay per hour. However the publication did get me much better known in the chemical community. Since the royalties coming in each year were split between the six authors, each would receive only a small amount of money, so we had agreed to Keith's suggestion that we would each be paid a one-off fee for our writing whilst I, as editor, would also get a smaller royalty on each book sold, sent to me annually.

Reviews of the book were invariably excellent and this led to one reviewer, Dr. Bryan Reuben, contacting me. He was organising an academic study tour of universities in Israel. The party consisted of UK university lecturers and professors teaching chemistry and chemical engineering. He had just one place left and offered it to me; quite an honour. My Head of Department, Dr Joe Fenerty, was very supportive and agreed that the department would pay for my air fares, and since all travel and accommodation in Israel was covered, I jumped at the chance.

I did not know any of the other members of our group of 15 but met them at Heathrow Airport ready for our flight to Tel Aviv. Following check-in and the extensive security checks (even in those days, for El Al flights) we were seated around the aircraft. Some four hours later the captain announced that we had just passed over the coast of Israel and many of the passengers started clapping, cheering and singing.

Our stay was mainly in top-class hotels, although we spent one night in a kibbutz near the Sea of Galilee, where, to my surprise, the accommodation was on a par with that in the hotels. It was interesting to see just what the members of the kibbutz had achieved through their joint efforts, with quite a variety of crops being grown, although the strict regime, with children being in nursery or school so their parents could work, would not have suited me. We visited several universities and received a warm and friendly welcome, but there was far too much food for me. During our week's stay we covered virtually the whole country, from the Golan Heights in the north to Beersheba, on the edge of the Negev Desert in the south. Only Eilat in the far south was not covered. It was very moving to visit such biblical sites as Bethlehem, Nazareth, Masada, the Church of the Nativity, the Golden Domed Al Aqsa Mosque and the Wailing or Western Wall. The golden dome was our exciting first view of Jerusalem in the distance. Our only regret was not having time to bathe in the very salty Dead Sea.

All this was accomplished in just a week, with our driver being armed and our guide a former Israeli Ambassador to Australia. We would never have guessed this from his demeanour, eg sitting up front with his feet on the dashboard of our mini-coach.

Our trip to the Desert Research Institute at Beersheba was interesting and informative. We were amazed to see oranges and other fruits growing on the edge of the desert, only because of the water piped hundreds of miles from the River Jordan to irrigate them. In fact it turned out that we had picked a unique day for our visit, with flash floods almost blocking our route back.

The most moving part of our trip was a visit to Yad Vashem, the memorial to the Holocaust, where a number of visitors, having lost relatives in the Holocaust, were totally overcome with emotion and were crying uncontrollably.

On our final evening, spent in Jerusalem, our guide took us to a night club owned by his singer girlfriend. She even managed to get some of our party up singing with her and then let slip that we were the guests of the Israeli Foreign

Ministry! No wonder all expenses were covered. These visits were immensely valuable for the local university staff, affording the opportunity for research collaborations to be initiated and mitigating their sense of isolation.

At one of the stalls, in the market in the old city in Jerusalem, I was contemplating buying bracelets with coloured stones for my wife and daughter. The trader held them out for me to see and they looked very nice. Having paid the Arab vendor I received my wrapped package, which went straight into my case at the hotel. On arriving home I gave the package to my wife, but was horrified when she opened it and I saw that broken bracelets had been substituted for the proper ones which I had been shown. To add insult to injury neither my daughter nor wife liked them anyway! This was the first time, and hopefully the last, I have been conned like this – a valuable lesson not to be so trusting in the future.

There was an interesting episode when Blackie's was approached by a film company which wanted to use my book as a prop in a scene in a cell where a prisoner serving a life sentence (Nicolas Cage) had become interested in science! We agreed, but were not offered any fee.

Keith and I had appreciated at an early stage that because of the vastness of the subject, a complementary book covering other areas would be needed. As a result *The Chemical Industry* was published in 1986, as a complementary volume to *An Introduction to Industrial Chemistry*. Although much basic material in the books changes very little over several years, some topics clearly do, eg statistics on the chemical industry, so periodically the books required updating. Although it was not as onerous as writing the first books, we decided that they would include some new topics and new authors, so teams had to be recruited. Another driving force for this was that some of the original authors had retired and were gradually becoming out of touch with new developments in their area. This resulted in the publication of a second edition of *An Introduction to Industrial Chemistry* in 1991 and a third in 1996. In between, in 1994, we produced the second edition of *The Chemical Industry*. Although I have not carried out any further work on the books since then, it is pleasing to report that even now (2017) I am still receiving royalties, albeit rather small ones. However a large German publisher, Springer, now owns the titles.

My very successful career continued on an upward trajectory with promotion to Senior Lecturer in Organic Chemistry, then Reader in Industrial Chemistry and finally, in 2002, to a personal chair as Professor of Chemical Education – not bad for an academic failure at school! I also became Head of Chemistry in the School of Pharmacy and Chemistry at Liverpool John Moores University. Amusingly, shortly after Liverpool Poly became this university, I was running a conference when one of my speakers arrived at Liverpool Lime Street station and asked a taxi driver to take him to the university. His reply, with typical Scouse humour, was "Is that the real university or the John?"!

Busy as I was in the 1980s and 1990s with all the activities described, in 1997 I was asked by the Royal Society of Chemistry to write a book entitled "Problem Solving in Analytical Chemistry". Their Education Officer, and a good friend of mine, Dr Neville Reed (with whom I had worked at many OU summer Schools at Nottingham University), was able to get the terms of a Trust Fund amended to pay for an assistant to help me. We invited all university chemistry departments in the UK to submit problems to us and then we chose the most suitable ones, put them in standard format and placed them in appropriate categories with the answers. After getting several colleagues in other universities to test them out, plus using them with my own students, we refined them and published the book in 1998. As a valuable teaching resource a complimentary copy was sent to every university chemistry department in the UK. It remained extremely important for several years, helping chemistry students to acquire one of the most important skills they need, ie the ability to solve problems. Unfortunately once Google etc arrived, rather than working out the answers the students could just look them up.

At this time, as well as a full teaching load and supervising the research of my PhD student, I had my usual heavy administrative load. This now included being Admissions Tutor (responsible for recruiting all the students for our chemistry courses), chairing the Research Committee for the School of Pharmacy & Chemistry and serving on the university's Research Committee. Surprisingly this was not a problem, because I really enjoyed what I was doing, and looked forward to going to work each day and teaching my students.

Our annual degree day was always a source of pride and satisfaction, with students thanking me for helping them to gain their degree and wanting me to pose with them and their families for photographs. The ceremonies were held in the magnificent setting of the Anglican Cathedral in Liverpool and the university had so many students graduating that ceremonies were held every morning and afternoon for a whole week. I used to really enjoy wearing the gown that went with my PhD in Science from Durham University, as it was a bright red colour. It always took me back to a few days after my doctorate was conferred and we showed our son, Simon (aged two), a photo of this and asked him who it was in the red gown and unusual black cap. Naturally we expected him to say Daddy, so we had a good laugh when he said Father Christmas!

At each ceremony a couple of notable persons received

honorary fellowships from the university. We were jealous of the media and arts schools, since their recipients were often TV or film stars like 'Mrs Bouquet' (Patricia Routledge), whereas ours were less well known (to the public) and sometimes rather dour scientists, although one year the Olympic wheelchair champion Tanni Grey-Thompson was a recipient. On another occasion it was the comedian Ken Dodd, shortly after he had been found not guilty in the courts of tax evasion. In his speech after receiving his award, which he managed to limit to 15 minutes after being told no more than 10, he said that he was now studying for his Master's degree in accountancy! After the ceremony I was most impressed at how long he stayed having his photograph taken with many of the graduands and their families. For the first few years all the fellowship recipients either came from Liverpool or had connections with it, including the Everton and Liverpool football clubs, but this requirement was then dropped.

After the Millennium my work as Professor of Chemical Education became gradually less enjoyable, with increasing numbers of students showing little interest in the course or subject. It was at this stage, much sooner than I had expected, that I began to contemplate retirement.

CHAPTER 10

INDUSTRIAL FELLOWSHIP AT ICI

In 1987 I had been at Liverpool almost 20 years and seen the Regional College of Technology, where I started, merge with other colleges in the city to become Liverpool Polytechnic. When I read that the Science and Engineering Research Council (SERC), which funded research in universities, was starting a scheme of Industrial Fellowships jointly with the Royal Society, I decided to find out more about them. Its aim was to enable academics to spend time working in industry, or industrialists to move into academia for a period. In reality it transpired that most of the movement involved academics going into industry. The fellowship supplied funding to provide teaching cover, whilst the academic became an employee of the company for the period of the fellowship. This was very much to the advantage of the academics, since industrial salaries were much higher.

For me it would be a chance to recharge my batteries and get back into research, without any distractions such as administrative duties. Having decided that I would apply for a fellowship, there were several factors to consider before starting discussions with a company that would support my application and host me. Firstly it would need to be a local company to which I could easily commute daily. Secondly their areas of research would need to be those with which I was familiar, ie my PhD or Poly projects.

The most suitable company was quickly identified as ICI Mond Division's research laboratories at The Heath in Runcorn. I knew them and many of the staff very well through several links. Ever since coming to Liverpool I had been teaching their employees on our part-time degree courses. A few of them were my colleagues on the SCI Liverpool Section Committee, and Dr Harold Fielding was one of my speakers on the SCI/LJMU Schools/Industry project. When I had discussed my plans with him he introduced me to his group leader, Dr John Beacham, and another member of the group, Dr Dick Powell, who I would work with on a joint project. With their support I applied for, and was delighted to gain, one of the five fellowships that were on offer.

At this time ICI had an enormous and growing group of scientists and engineers (over 100) who were trying to discover and develop replacements for CFCs (chlorofluorocarbons). These were immensely important chemicals which were used as refrigerants, foam-blowing agents (in things like expanded polystyrene, where they are trapped as a gas inside the polymer), and are best known to the public as propellants in aerosols containing deodorants, hairspray etc. After many years of research they had been implicated in destroying some of the ozone layer in the stratosphere which shields us from the dangerous short wavelength UV-B rays. This could lead to a large increase in the number of skin cancer cases. Following an international agreement (the Montreal Protocol) to limit their use and phase them out, replacements had to be developed to allow this. The British Government, led by Margaret Thatcher, was pushing the timetable further forward, putting even greater pressure on ICI and others. This is discussed in more detail in Chapter 15.

So in 1988 I became an ICI employee for a year, working on a part of the above project. As indicated earlier, since industrial salaries were much higher than those in academia, I was able to negotiate a significant increase. For the first time in over 20 years I had to have a medical examination and was told I needed reading glasses. The doctor, seeing me looking crestfallen, tried to comfort me by saying "don't worry it is only your age"! On the plus side she told me that my lung capacity was much higher than expected; not surprising since I went swimming at the baths near the Poly three lunchtimes per week. Still ICI paid for the spectacles, since I would be using them in the laboratory.

In the research laboratory where I worked the person who was in charge of Health and Safety was a former student of mine, so in this area he was my boss. Being back at the bench was initially challenging, but well worth it, and it would result the following year in the company making a European and US patent application for a new method we had developed. This was for introducing a trifluoromethyl (CF_3) group into aromatic molecules. This was of particular interest because a number of new drugs and pesticides contained this group in their chemical structures and the method could be used to make new molecules that might show similar, or even better, activity. Due to the success of my work the fellowship was extended from 12 to 15 months.

In September 1989 I was able to present a paper to report these results at the International Fluorine Conference at Leicester University. Dick Powell also encouraged me to visit other ICI sites to talk about my research. These included Jealott's Hill in Berkshire (now Syngenta) where potential new pesticides were discovered, developed and tested, both in the laboratory and on crops in the surrounding fields. I also went to Grangemouth in Scotland, where the R&D Department was attached to the refinery. This was in the news in 2015 when the refinery almost closed, but was rescued when the trade unions finally agreed to the proposals of the new owners, Ineos. A key sticking point had been the company's plan to import ethane in refrigerated tanker ships from the USA, where it had been produced by the fracking of shale. Even after the transportation costs this was still the cheapest source. The ethane is fed into giant catalytic crackers, where at high temperature it is converted into ethylene and propylene. These in turn are the building blocks for many polymers, eg polythene.

Travel was a markedly different experience from that when on Polytechnic business. Here I was collected from home, driven to Manchester airport and on arrival at Edinburgh airport a chauffeur was waiting to take me to Grangemouth, with similar arrangements for the return journey.

At this time ICI was probably the fourth largest chemical company in the world and very profitable, so employees were treated very generously. Hence any chemicals, or new specialist equipment, were readily sanctioned and permission to attend any relevant conferences, with generous travel and accommodation expenses, was easily obtained. I was the beneficiary of this generosity and largesse during the latter part of my time there. In late 1989 I was invited to become the next Chairman of the Liverpool Section of SCI. Shortly afterwards I was approached by the current Chairman of the RSC Liverpool Section, Dr David Nicholls, and asked to become their next Chairman. Despite protesting that I was already committed to the SCI role he still wanted me to go ahead. So for one crazy year I was Chairman of the Liverpool Sections of both societies – the first and last person ever to do so!

How does this relate to ICI? Well, they had a special dining room for visitors where pre-lunch drinks were followed with wine plus a sumptuous lunch. I had lots of RSC and SCI visitors, so I would be there at least once a week entertaining my guests. In fact when I left to return to the Polytechnic one of my ICI colleagues joked that the visitors' restaurant would now have to close down due to the drop in clientele. Looking back, and bearing in mind the much greater emphasis now on health and safety, it seems almost criminal that after several drinks we went back in the afternoon to continue working in the laboratory and handling some incredibly dangerous chemicals, eg hydrofluoric acid, one drop of which if spilled on your skin will burn down to the bone in a matter of seconds. Nowadays, of course, this would not be tolerated and entertaining visitors to lunch on site is 'dry', ie with alcohol not permitted. However most of my visitors had little to do with ICI.

I was also able to get generous support from the company, mainly through John Beacham, for activities for SCI in particular. These included holding meetings on site (free of charge), supporting my schools/industry project and holding a prestigious dinner at the company's Lawson House. This was for the presentation of SCI's Lampitt Medal for outstanding service, to Dr Don Broad and Professor Dick Hamilton, both of whom were members of the Liverpool Section. This was the first time that the event had been held outside the society's London Headquarters, so it represented quite a coup for me. Even better, SCI never received a bill! John also instituted an annual student prize at Liverpool Poly.

On a personal note I also gained an SERC CASE PhD studentship jointly with ICI, with Dick Powell as the second supervisor of my student. A few years later we persuaded John Beacham to join SCI and he rapidly became Chairman of Council, and later, President of the society.

In 2005 Dick and I were invited to be co-guest editors of a special issue of the international Journal of Fluorine Chemistry, which was devoted to industrial aspects of the subject. Before this we had joined with a friend of mine, Dr Tina Overton of Hull University, to devise a problem-based learning package entitled "The Challenge to Develop CFC

Replacements". Tina and I used it in our teaching of Industrial Chemistry modules on our BSc (Hons) courses for several years.

CHAPTER 11

MY CONTRIBUTIONS TO THE LEARNED SOCIETIES IN CHEMISTRY

In the UK there are two learned societies in Chemistry, although they are very much international societies with branches throughout the world. They are the Royal Society of Chemistry (RSC) and the Society of Chemical Industry (SCI). Both are long established, with the RSC tracing its roots back over more than 175 years and SCI over 135 years. Both have their headquarters in London, Burlington House in Piccadilly and Belgrave Square respectively, although most RSC staff now work in their offices in Cambridge. They are both registered charities.

The RSC is the professional body for chemists, and to

become a member requires the necessary qualifications, although in recent years the requirements have been eased a little so that other scientists practising chemistry can join as Associate Members. It has almost 50,000 members, and even though almost a quarter work in the chemical and related industries, its council and committees are dominated by academics. Full details are available at www.rsc.org .

In contrast no qualifications are needed in order to join SCI, merely an interest in the application of chemistry and related sciences for the benefit of society. Its membership is very broad and it is the only truly multi-disciplinary learned society in Europe with its members covering virtually all sciences, engineering and business; in fact its strapline is "where science meets business". It was set up in the mid-1800s by captains of industry and, in contrast to RSC, its Board of Trustees and committees are predominantly filled by industrialists and business people, plus some academics. Its membership base is very much smaller at around 3,000 but it includes a number of senior industrialists. Full details are available at www.soci.org.

My lifelong association with the two societies began during my college studies. In 1961, in order to sit the external exams to gain my Grad.RIC, I had to join the Royal Institute of Chemistry (the forerunner of RSC) as a student member. This qualification is equivalent to a first or upper second class BSc (Hons) degree in Chemistry. Shortly after gaining this qualification I became an Associate Member (ARIC) and several years later, after suitable professional experience, a Fellow (FRSC).

In the 1970s I joined the Liverpool Section Committee of RSC, and would continue on it for over 20 years, serving as Chairman in 1990-1991. At a regional level I joined the North West Trust Committee in 1993 and remained on it until the trust was wound up in 2015. For many years the RSC Manchester Section had run a big exhibition of laboratory equipment each year, and the companies paid for a stand from which they promoted and sold their wares. It therefore made a good profit (or surplus, since it is a charity) and when the exhibition (Labex) was sold to a commercial company, all the remaining funds were put into the North West Trust and could be used to support educational projects related to chemistry and industry. It was therefore an excellent committee to be a member of, since all we did was to give away money to support good projects.

Throughout the 1990s and 2000s I was very active on national and international committees based at RSC's headquarters at Burlington House in London. These included serving as an elected member of the governing body, the Council (1994-1997), and the Research Committee (2005-2010). I also served three terms as an elected member of the Education Division Council (1990-1993, 2005-2008 and 2008-2011) and was asked to chair its Higher Education

Sub-Committee (1990-1993). As in all my committee work I was a very active member, serving on working parties and organising events. The latter included twice organising a two-day international education conference at the RSC's annual meeting.

At one stage I was invited to join the national organising and co-ordinating committee for Chemistry Week. This is held in November in each year and local sections and members organise events to promote the excitement and fun of chemistry to young people and the public, with demonstrations often held in places like shopping malls. We decided that we needed a big national event in London that would attract lots of media interest and gain us lots of publicity, to launch the week. Our idea was to get the TV celebrity and magician Paul Daniels to give a chemistry presentation and demonstration. We would write the script and organise the demonstrations and Paul would come along and have an hour's rehearsal before the actual event.

We were rather shocked when his agent wanted to charge us £1,000 – a lot of money in the early 1980s and way beyond our budget. So we put on our thinking caps and I was delighted when my colleagues accepted my suggestion that instead we should invite my friend Dr Brian Iddon to give his well-known lecture/demonstration "The Magic of Chemistry". Brian and I had worked together at both Durham and Salford Universities, and after a long career at the latter he was elected as an MP for one of the Bolton constituencies. My wife Joy and I were in the audience when he did the show at the Royal Institution, a venue he had always wanted to perform at – and he only cost us his travelling expenses!

Finally in 2014 I received my certificate to celebrate 50 years of RSC membership. For the past 15 to 20 years my efforts have been much more focused on the Society of Chemical Industry (SCI, www.soci.org). As indicated earlier, I joined SCI in 1973 and served on the Liverpool Section Committee from then until it ceased to exist following a merger with the Manchester Section in 2006. My record includes serving as Chairman a unique three times (1989-1991, 1996-1999 and 2005-2006); even the three Lord Leverhulmes only served one term each! In fact in 1991, with Sir Geoffrey Allen and other senior Unilever staff, I organised a special event at the Grosvenor Hotel in Chester to celebrate the centenary of the first Viscount Leverhulme joining SCI. Many senior industrialists and academics from the region plus the Lord Mayor of Chester attended. However I had to delay the start of the meeting for the arrival of our special guest – the current Lord Leverhulme. He was late because he had been entertaining the Queen on her visit to Cheshire, in his role as Lord Lieutenant of the County. I advised the assembled audience that although we knew the whereabouts of the first Lord Leverhulme, we were not so sure about the current one!

Over the years I have led the organisation of a number of prestigious lectures, particularly our endowed Hurter and Leverhulme ones. Speakers included Sir Geoffrey Allen, Baroness Susan Greenfield, Lord Porter, and Sir Geoffrey Wilkinson. The latter two were each awarded the Nobel Prize in Chemistry. After the lecture there was a dinner for invited guests, which we used to facilitate interaction between senior academics and industrialists from the North West region.

When the Liverpool and Manchester sections merged to form the Liverpool & North West Regional Interest Group, my colleagues afforded me the honour of inviting me to be the first Chair. By then I was already on several SCI national/international committees, which met at the society's headquarters in Belgrave Square, London. These included the Awards Committee (1995-2005), the Messel & Gray Scholarship & Travel Bursary Selection Committee (1996-2006) and chairing the Distinguished Service Award Panel (2000-2006). I was also a member of the governing body, the SCI Council (1989-1991, 1996-2002 and 2004-2007). Following a governance reorganisation in 2007 the Council was replaced by a Board of Trustees (BoT), with most of its membership being directly elected by the members. In 2015 I was re-elected for a third three-year term.

My links with university students and 'early career people', as people on the first rungs of their careers are now known, have been enhanced through SCI, especially since I took early retirement from LJMU in 2005, and this work now takes up quite a lot of my time. Following a major review of Awards and the Awards Committee in 2009, BoT decided to disband the latter and replace it with a sub-committee of the board called the 'Early Career Support Sub-Committee' (ECSSC); rather a mouthful and all to be politically correct by avoiding the term young in the title! I was invited to chair it. Along with this the SCI College of Scholars was set up in 2009 to support holders of the prestigious SCI Scholarships (three per year) and I was asked to be the Honorary Principal. I am still continuing in both these roles today, although ECSSC has been renamed SCI Early Careers Committee (ECC). ECC has delegated responsibility for choosing the three scholars each year and also awarding around about 40 travel bursaries per year. Applicants for the scholarships are invariably academically outstanding, having not only a first class BSc (Hons) or Master's degree, but being in the top few of the cohort of students on their course. Travel bursaries are awarded to science and engineering PhD students to help cover the costs of them attending a conference to present a paper or poster on their research work or making a visit to another institution to gain additional experience, or using specialist equipment. Why is it that nowadays so many of these conferences seem to be held in Hawaii or Los Angeles?

Although last year we did make an award to someone presenting a paper at a conference in Sheffield! Marking all these applications (each several full pages long) is a time-consuming but enjoyable experience. ECC also has responsibility for driving all early career events and initiatives from the society's London Headquarters. It organises major careers events each year plus a Conference Day for SCI scholars, ambassadors and early career people serving on the society's committees. We have also recently launched a mentoring scheme. Little wonder I am so busy!

People ask why I spend all this time voluntarily on SCI activities. I do it firstly because I enjoy doing it and secondly because most of the people I work with are really good and friendly people, even if a few are a pain in the ****! Thirdly, it is a chance to interact with people from disciplines other than chemistry. Finally, it is an opportunity for me to put something back and help early career people after all the benefits I have gained from being a professional chemist, although I am only half joking when I say that I took early retirement from LJMU so that I could work for SCI! I am also passionate about my subject, which is why I have spent so much of my life promoting it to children, young people and the public.

All my contributions to SCI were formally acknowledged in 2004 when I was awarded the society's prestigious Lampitt Medal. This is awarded to someone who has given outstanding service to the society over many years and in several areas of its interests. Only one medal is awarded each year, sometimes none at all.

CHAPTER 12

DRAMA ON A MOUNTAIN PEAK

This story really had its origins several years earlier in Scotland, where I was teaching at an Open University Science Foundation Course Summer School at Stirling University. This has been described fully in chapter 8.

One of the Course Director's key jobs was to get all 20 tutors working as a team, and this was facilitated by everyone having a quick drink together in between finishing the afternoon lab session and going to dinner before the tutorials started. It also enabled any problems which had occurred to be discussed and sorted out. Wednesday afternoons and evenings were free and groups of tutors (and students) played golf, climbed the hills behind the university, visited the Wallace Monument or went swimming in the university swimming pool. This fostered great camaraderie amongst the tutors, which was reinforced by some being allocated the same week for several years running. I formed some great friendships which continue to this day and some, sadly, with colleagues who have since passed away.

One of these was Dr Audrey Brown, who was teaching Biology whilst I was teaching Chemistry. We remain friends to this day, although contact now is largely via Christmas cards. She and her family had moved up to near Barrow-in-Furness when her husband, Chris, was appointed by the Royal Navy as Weapons Systems Officer to the nuclear submarine HMS Trafalgar being built at VSEL, and on which he would serve once it was launched. At this time I was Professional Training Tutor for the Chemistry Courses at Liverpool Polytechnic, so I had the job of placing all students with an industrial company for the whole of the third year of their four-year sandwich course. Hence I was always looking for contacts in companies. A few OU students who Audrey taught in her local group worked for chemical firms and she was able to introduce me to them, resulting in placements for some of my students. When I visited them we would meet up for a chat and we also overlapped at a few later OU Summer Schools.

On the 22nd February 2001 I had been invited by the

Royal Society of Chemistry's Cumbria Section to give my talk on "Pesticides in Perspective" to their evening meeting in Whitehaven. This covered discussing 'problem' pesticides like DDT (discussed in Chapter 15) and Agent Orange but concentrated on the discovery and development of new pesticides, now referred to as 'plant protection agents' by the agrochemical industry because of the unfavourable press the word 'pesticide' attracted just because a few caused problems. Since I was staying there overnight I had previously contacted Audrey to see if she would like to do some mountain walking the next day. We decided to attempt to climb England's highest mountain, Scafell Pike (3, 210 feet) in the western part of the Lake District, and arranged to meet at the foot of it at 9.15.

The day started quite cold but bright and I enjoyed the drive down the Cumbrian coast, and then inland along the side of Wastwater, which is England's deepest lake at 258 feet. We duly met in the car park at about 9.15, and after putting on anoraks, hats, gloves, climbing boots and backpacks we started the climb at 9.30. It was a reasonably clear day, although there was a light dusting of snow on the ground. After an hour of steady climbing we stopped for a hot drink and some food. After a further hour of solid effort we reached Mickledore Ridge, which links the peaks of Scafell and Scafell Pike and is at an altitude of

2, 745 feet. There had been a few small snow flurries

during this time with the temperature around freezing.

Now ready to start the final ascent, we passed a mountain rescue kit box. Little did we realise what a significant part it would play over the next few hours.

As we headed left, at about 11.30, we thought we heard a faint voice behind us crying "help me, you have got to help me!" We retraced our steps and although we could not see anyone, we could hear a man shouting that he had fallen and was seriously injured with broken bones. Audrey climbed back onto the ridge in order to get a mobile phone signal and call the police, whilst I descended the scree slope. I discovered the casualty below the cliffs of Broad Stand, noting that there was ice on many parts of the cliffs.

I shouted up to Audrey that the injured person could not move because of the pain and I thought he had broken his right arm and leg; also there was blood seeping out of his walking boot. She passed this information on to the police, and the mountain rescue kit box was a valuable reference point to guide the mountain rescue team to our location. We later learned that the spot where the accident had happened had been the location of a number of such incidents and as a result, as soon as the mountain rescue team learned of it they immediately requested that a rescue helicopter be dispatched from RAF Boulmer in Northumberland, 40 minutes' flying time away.

Amazingly, when the 999 call was first answered and

Audrey described the emergency, before the operator put her through to the police, she asked if Audrey had called an ambulance! Maybe in Cumbria they have wings!

I established that the injured man's name was Andrew Robson, he was the Bridge Correspondent for *The Times* newspaper, and that he had been enjoying a break in the Lake District with his family, since he was a keen and experienced fell walker. I covered him with my fleece and leggings. The temperature was now below zero. He could not be moved because of the pain and the worry that doing so might cause more injuries. Audrey found a large fleecy sleeping bag and a plastic tent in the mountain rescue kit box, and we covered him with these. She returned up onto the ridge to await any phone calls from the police.

I was concerned to make sure Andrew kept awake, and whilst chatting to him I found that he had been trying to climb down the cliffs (the guide books suggest you should not even attempt this descent in summer) and had slipped on the ice and fallen onto the rocks below and then onto the scree slope where he now lay – a total fall of about 20 metres. He thought that we had found him about 20 minutes after he fell. His trousers were ripped and it was already quite cold.

The rest of the drama unfolded as follows (times are approximate):

12.00: Members of the Wasdale Mountain Rescue Team

are bleeped at work. One member, Richard Warren, was in a meeting at Sellafield when he was buzzed, but he made it to the foot of the mountain in 40 minutes despite having to drive along narrow country lanes for more than 20 miles.

Our challenge was to keep Andrew warm and awake, although I was concerned that we could not get anything warm under him since he was laid on cold, bare rock and scree. We gave him hot tea and he managed to eat a Mars bar.

12.30: Another fell walker, Peter Corrigan, arrives on the scene with his dog Barney. He has some ibuprofen with him and gives Andrew two. We keep talking to him to ensure he stays awake, but note his right sock is soaked in blood. We marvel at how well he is coping with the pain and he thanks us several times for saving his life. Several snow flurries.

13.40: The first member of the mountain rescue team arrives and advises the other members of the team of the situation by radio.

13:50: The first doctor arrives and administers diamorphine to ease the pain. He is soon followed by more team members, including two doctors. They give Andrew oxygen and are very concerned to treat his ankle and leg injuries quickly. The ankle is badly broken and his leg has a compound fracture. Inflatable splints are fitted and he is lifted onto a vacuum mattress. A heart rate monitor is unpacked and attached to him.

14:15: A Sea King helicopter arrives. Because of the

wind and proximity of the cliffs it cannot land nearby, only on a flat area higher up the mountain. The two halves of a metal stretcher are taken from the mountain rescue kit box and Andrew is carefully placed on it. The rescue team has now grown to 14, and 10 of these carry the stretcher up the steep and slippery scree slope. Two are stationed above, belaying ropes which are tied to the stretcher. The carry is 1,000 metres with 200 metres of ascent.

15.00: The stretcher is placed on the helicopter, which lifts off and swoops away for the short journey to the nearby West Cumberland Hospital in Whitehaven. We say our goodbyes to the mountain rescue team and debate whether or not we have time to climb to the summit and get back down to our cars before darkness falls. Our decision is to go for it, and accompanied by Peter and his dog Barney, we make the summit and briefly look at the views from the highest point in England before a rapid descent gets us to the car park at the foot of the mountain just as dusk descends.

After farewells to Peter and Barney we drove towards Ulverston, where our routes diverged. Audrey had a short drive home, but I still had a 100-mile drive ahead of me. I made my way across the southern Lake District via Newby Bridge to the M6, and by the time I reached the services south of Lancaster I was ready for a break. It was only when I began to ponder over my fish and chips, the enormity of what had happened dawned on me, along with some 'what ifs'.

What if we had proceeded straight from the ridge to the summit?

What if we had not heard Andrew's cries?

What if there had not been vital materials in the nearby mountain rescue kit box?

The outcome would have been tragically different and Andrew almost certainly would have died from hypothermia. Fortunately there was a much happier outcome. After several weeks and several operations in the West Cumbria Hospital, Andrew was moved to one nearer home in the south of England. More operations were needed before he made a good recovery.

We wrote a short account of the rescue for the Wasdale Mountain Rescue website and Peter Corrigan provided his photographs of the rescue to accompany it – you can see the report at http://www.wmrt.org.uk/incidents/incident-08-in-2001/.

Richard Warren of the mountain rescue team commented: "Two of the three experienced walkers were at the right place at the right time and did the right thing. Their alertness, level headedness and selfless care for a fellow walker undoubtedly saved his life. Friday, 23rd February 2001 will remain a memorable day for them all. We will also remember it as the day we carried the casualty up the mountain rather than down".

What we should all learn from the above story is that to enjoy the beautiful scenery and mountain climbing in the Lake District we should plan and act carefully, and always try to embark on mountain climbing with at least one companion. The weather conditions can change so quickly even in summer, and more so in winter.

CHAPTER 13

Retirement, and setting up a BSc course in Oman

I have explained how after the Millennium, my work as Professor of Chemical Education became gradually less enjoyable and rewarding, with a growing number of students showing less and less interest. By this time the courses were broken down into modules and some of these students deliberately worked only, and then moderately, in about half of the modules, just scraping a pass. They knew that for the remaining modules (which they had failed) they would be set some work to do and be offered resits. Usually they managed to scrape through these, although their mark was capped at the minimum pass of 40%. However this allowed them to proceed on to the next year of the course. This was undoubtedly a consequence of the Labour government ruling that the proportion of young people going to university should be increased to 50%. Since many of the most able young people had already qualified to attend university clearly many of the additional students were less academically suitable and so would obviously struggle to complete the course. The most important aspect, that students starting the courses should be able to cope and benefit, was ignored. The consequence since then has, in my opinion been, that courses have been made easier e.g. many more people graduating now gain 1sts or 2:1s.

Finally these changes, coupled with some sad news nearer home, led me to a momentous decision. In 2005 my next-door neighbour and good friend Brian developed cancer of the oesophagus. He had only been retired for a short time when he was diagnosed in October , and the following February he died. I had also seen a few of my colleagues enjoy only a year or two's retirement before they passed away.

Joy could hardly believe me when I informed her that I had decided to retire a few years early. We had always both thought I would have to be dragged out of the door kicking and screaming when my retirement date came.

And so ended 36 years working at LJMU and its predecessors. A bonus was persuading my Head of

Department, Professor Jim Ford, to make me redundant, and the additional payments covered the costs of our daughter's wedding.

For a few years afterwards I continued to recruit for, and teach on, the summer top-up course in Biology and Chemistry which I had helped to set up a few years earlier. This was for students from Tunku Abdul Raman (TAR) College in Kuala Lumpur (KL) in Malaysia. One year Joy was able to join me on the trip to KL to recruit the students, and we managed to fit in a visit to Singapore to see her niece and family first. Engineering courses for TAR students had been set up a few years earlier than ours, but by now several different courses were running, right across the university.

All of this was most enjoyable, firstly because our 20th floor hotel room in KL looked out directly on to the twin towers of the famous Petronas Building, which is probably the best-known tourist sight in the city. Secondly, in addition to recruiting for the forthcoming summer courses at LJMU, a degree ceremony was held for the students who had completed the course the previous summer, which enabled their families to share in their success and see them receive their degree certificates from our Vice-Chancellor. Over 300 students attended the ceremony. I am immensely proud of the fact that over the several years that I taught on the TAR course EVERY student passed – testament to the ability, hard work and commitment of all the students and the excellence of the teaching that we provided. In fact even though classes were timetabled almost all day from Monday to Friday, on only a couple of occasions can I remember any student missing a class, even though some might come in coughing and spluttering. Their tremendous commitment was down to their knowledge of the financial sacrifice that most of their families were making to send them on the course, and also knowing the great value and esteem that a UK university degree would have back home in Malaysia. We also arranged social events for the students, such as guided walks around the city and walls in Chester, and lunch and a tour of the Anfield stadium of Liverpool FC. This reminds me that when we were recruiting the students in KL we always asked them what they knew about Liverpool. The answers, invariably, were that it was cold and Liverpool were a great football team. In fairness we had to point out that there was another great team in the city called Everton! What a pity more of my full-time UK students could not show the same commitment. By 2010 their college in KL had been awarded degree-giving powers, so the courses in Liverpool were no longer needed.

Early in 2006 I received an email from a Professor Mohammed Khan, Head of the Chemistry Department at Sultan Qaboos University (SQU) in Muscat, Oman, asking me if I would review their proposal for a BSc (Hons) course in Applied (Industrial) Chemistry. This would complement the existing Chemistry degree which had been running since the university started in 1986. I sent my comments, which he thanked me for.

Wondering why he had contacted me, I came to two conclusions. Firstly he and his colleagues had probably seen the textbooks which I had written and which fitted the course. Secondly a colleague of mine at LJMU had moved to SQU a few years after it opened and he had, no doubt, recommended me.

I heard nothing further and I was wondering if I should request payment for my time and effort, but decided not to. During the summer I received another email asking me if I would take on the position of Visiting Consultant in the department, to advise them on setting up the new course, and also do some teaching on the existing chemistry course. They wanted me to go for the spring semester (January-June) in 2007. Since we knew hardly anything about Oman, we quickly got some guide books out of the local library and my wife and I agreed that it would be an exciting and new experience, so I accepted.

We corresponded by email for several months in sorting out the contract (I agreed to give some additional seminars to the teaching staff, which enabled Professor Khan to get the university to agree to a higher salary than they had originally offered) and I was getting concerned that things had still not been finalised, but I was assured that everything would be fine – 'Inshallah', which means God willing! In fact I received final confirmation only on Christmas Day in a phone call from the Professor's wife, who was a lecturer at Cambridge University.

Within a few weeks my wife and I were on an Emirates flight from Manchester to Dubai, where we would change planes for the short hop to Muscat in Oman. In Arab countries the weekend is Friday (their holy day) and Saturday, so we chose to fly out overnight on Thursday, giving us Friday and Saturday to settle in and get our bearings before I started work on the Sunday. Unfortunately the flight to Dubai was delayed, so we missed our connecting flight. We had not exchanged phone numbers with staff at SQU and so could not advise them of our situation. Our arrival in Muscat therefore mirrored our arrival in Kuala Lumpur years earlier, but in addition to us not knowing where we were to go, there was no one to meet us.

Professor Khan and Dr John Williams (an English member of the department's staff) had been at the airport waiting to greet us, and when we did not show they had gone home. Since it was the weekend we had great difficulty in contacting anyone at the university, but with the help of a friendly visa official, university transport for us was arranged and about an hour later our driver arrived. The driver dropped us off at the two-bedroomed house on the campus that was to be our home and I asked him to come back in an hour and take us shopping to the nearest supermarket (which turned out to be five miles away). He failed to return, but fortunately one of our new neighbours agreed to take us; he turned out to be the Head of the Chemical Engineering Department and I would later be having discussions with him about his department teaching some modules on our new course.

Having not had any sort of briefing, my first lecture was an eye opener. I arrived some 10 minutes before the start time, and shortly afterwards young women started filing in from a door at the rear of the classroom. They all wore the black burqa, covering them from head to toe, although they were not allowed to cover their faces. A few minutes before the start time the boys, most wearing white dishdashers, filed in through the front door.

This segregation also occurred in the laboratory classes. As a result I had to give my introductory briefing at the start twice, at one end to the boys and then a repeat performance at the other end to the girls. There were even separate balance rooms, where they went to weigh out the chemicals, for the sexes.

It was in the lab that I accidentally committed a mortal sin, in the Omanis' eyes! I was talking to a female student next to the fume hood and at the front of it was a steam bath. As we continued chatting she was edging slowly backwards. Realising that she was in danger of burning herself on the hot bath, my natural reaction was to put my arm on her back and ease her forward, which I did. The next day one of my female Omani colleagues (who had studied in the USA, and met her future English husband there) found it very embarrassing to tell me that touching an Arab woman was an absolute no-no in their culture.

I immediately went to appraise the Head of Department, Professor Khan (who was a Muslim, but from Bangladesh), of the situation. He had gained his PhD at Cambridge University and went back there each summer to collaborate on research, so he was fairly relaxed about the incident and told me not to worry about it. However when the student feedback forms on our teaching came in, all the female students had included a comment that I had touched the female student! This was in contrast to all the other feedback during my time at SQU, which was very complementary and positive.

SQU took only Omanis as students and they had all studied English in school, although, as you would expect, their ability to speak and write it varied quite a lot. This worked to their advantage, because when marking their assignments and exam papers I made a generous allowance for the fact that English was their second language. By our standards their financial support was exceedingly generous, with no tuition fees, all accommodation and food paid for, and all textbooks available on loan for the whole semester.

The students were all extremely hard working and pleasant to teach and I was particularly pleased that I fairly quickly got them to come out of their shells and ask questions in the classroom. They were excellent at memorising facts (which they were used to), but it was quite a challenge to get them to think and develop their problem-solving skills. They had a very full curriculum with classes timetabled from 8 am to 6 pm, six days a week. They knew that the top few students at the end of the course would be invited to join the teaching staff where, after a few years' experience, they would be sent abroad (usually to the UK or USA, or increasingly to Australia) to study for a Master's Degree. Other jobs would be hard to come by. As a result it was very irritating when they would come to my office and spend half an hour arguing about one mark – if I let them. In my classes at this time, there was probably a 60:40 ratio of male to female students, although this would change significantly in my later visits.

Staffing was interesting, in that only five of the 25 staff were Omanis and six staff were visiting consultants, like me, although from India and other Middle Eastern countries. Alongside the teaching (only about 12 hours per week for me) I was leading six colleagues to develop and refine the syllabus for the new degree course, heavily influenced by my textbooks, which of course would be the recommended books for the course!

Our house on the campus was only 10 minutes' walk from the chemistry department, as was the staff club. The latter housed a gym, lounge, restaurant and an Olympic-sized swimming pool surrounded by sun loungers. There were also squash and tennis courts. It had been built by the British, originally for those building the new campus, and had a bar. Since they left it has not been used and is firmly padlocked. Most mornings I would go to the gym and then the pool before walking to my office. My wife could enjoy the gym and then the sun loungers, where she was often the only person there, except at the weekends. Temperatures started at around mid 20°C in January but had climbed above 35°C by the time we left in June, and we had virtually no rain at all.

Alcohol was only available in hotels and restaurants, so we ate out a couple of times a week. The university was beyond the airport right at the western end of Muscat, whereas most of the best eating places were 25-plus kilometres away at the eastern end. We had heard tales of people being arrested by the police for driving with alcohol in the boot of their car, or for drink driving, and immediately being taken to the airport and deported. However we did meet an American lecturer at the university who had twice been caught but let off! Interestingly, non-Muslims entering Oman are allowed to take in a case of beer or a couple of litres of spirits for personal use.

I would not drive to the restaurants, so we had to take taxis each time. Although a significant distance was involved the fares were very reasonable and we got very friendly with our regular taxi driver. He worked during the day as an ambulance driver at the university hospital. At his home, as well as his family, he had a camel which he raced and he was telling us about a camel 'beauty' show in Dubai where the winner received £100,000!

We returned home at the end of my contract having had an enjoyable, exciting and eye-opening six months. Some months later it was a very pleasant surprise to receive an email inviting me to return to SQU for the same spring semester in 2008. This was to do rather more teaching and complete the writing and checking of the new Applied Chemistry course ready for its submission for approval by the university. Construction of a new building for the Faculty of Science, next to the existing one, had also started, so I would be able to have some input into the design of the new laboratories. Fortunately one of my colleagues, who may have suspected that I would be invited back, had stored all our household utensils etc, and we were also able to re-engage our young Bangladeshi cleaner, who came in half a day each week to clean our house and do the washing and ironing. In fact on one occasion he told my wife off for doing the ironing, which he said was his job! With it being so hot there washing was dry within an hour of being hung on the line. It was again very enjoyable and we were able to eat out regularly, have weekends away (see chapter 14) and still save a good portion of my salary. My wife again returned home for four weeks in the middle because she was missing our children and grandchildren.

Now that the course was up and running and they were recruiting additional staff to teach it, I assumed that my visits to SQU were over, so it was quite a surprise when I received an email from Professor Majekodunmi Fatope, who had taken over as Head of the Chemistry Department, inviting me to be a visiting consultant for the autumn semester (August to January) in 2011, but the role would be to teach only. This was because they had now reached the final year of the Applied Chemistry course, where the teaching becomes more advanced and specialised, and they did not have the staff with the necessary expertise to cover some topics. I was happy to accept and the course leader was keen to stress that I should leave my lecture notes behind when I left.

The trip did not start well. Fortunately I had gone out a few weeks ahead of my wife. Despite my request for a house on the campus again, we were given a flat in the local town, which was several miles from the university, although transport was provided. I would be hiring a car again anyway. My main concern was that this would leave my wife rather isolated and unable to utilise the facilities of the staff club, and it would be more difficult for me to pop home at lunch time, as I had always done. The flat also had quite a few cockroaches, which I soon eliminated. After much pressing of the university administrators I managed to get us a house on the campus just before Joy arrived. However to add insult to injury it had not been cleaned since the previous occupants had left, so we had to set to and clean it ourselves. Ironically some weeks later we bumped into the Bangladeshi house boy who had worked for us on our previous visits. He was most aggrieved to learn that a colleague had already fixed us up with a new cleaner.

There were lots of difficulties with the teaching this time, and I seemed to be constantly thinking fast on my feet to resolve problems. This was mainly due to things not being done when I had said they must be done when I left in 2008. Firstly, the laboratory experiments had been checked by a technician (which I had said was essential), but he had been allowed to leave without reporting his findings and, particularly, any snags. Secondly some essential equipment which I needed for practically every experiment was not available, so I was constantly trying to think of ways round this. Thirdly I had recommended that staff must build strong links with local industry for collaboration and hosting works visits – an important part of an Applied or Industrial Chemistry course. Nothing had been done about that, so I had to start from scratch and try and arrange these visits with little or no knowledge of the companies, apart from the chemical area they worked in.

They proved to be something of a nightmare. On one occasion the university withdrew the transport at the last minute. Having set up another visit by phone and email we duly arrived to discover that they had no knowledge of our planned visit. Apparently the works manager with whom I had set up the visit had gone back home to India on holiday without telling any of his staff. However his colleagues did rally round and organise a reasonable tour for us. Leaving with complementary toiletries made the students a lot happier. In contrast to my earlier visits, where there was a slight predominance of male students, now one class was entirely female and the other had only five males in a class of 40 people.

My wife again went home for a month in the middle period, and I went on a couple of exciting and very enjoyable trips. Firstly the university organised two or three weekend trips for staff and their families each semester. The one I joined went for an overnight stay in the Wahiba Sands, where from the top of the dunes I witnessed glorious sunsets and sunrises, had a ride on a camel and sped up the dunes on a quad bike, my first experience on one. However the accommodation was more like that found in a three-star hotel.

My most memorable excursion was with my colleague

Dr John Williams. John was a very keen fisherman, and once each month he would hire a boat and skipper to go fishing in the Gulf of Oman. He would generously invite a colleague to join him. Whilst my wife was back in the UK he invited me to join him, even though my total fishing experience was a few hours in Florida whilst on a family holiday. We set off in the early morning and drove the 25 kilometres to the marina, located near the old city of Muscat, and set sail for our morning's fishing; it would be too hot in the afternoon. We followed dolphins which were chasing a school of tuna, which in turn were leaping spectacularly out of the water to avoid being eaten. This was an amazing sight, with over 100 dolphins visible. After about two hours we finally got a bite on the rod and line and John reeled in a nice tuna. It probably weighed about 1kg, and we would later eat it for supper.

Some 20 minutes later we were about to turn round to head back to port when there was another bite. It was my turn to hold the rod and follow John's instructions on what to do to slowly reel in the fish. After 10 minutes my arms were aching, so John took over, and later handed the rod back to me again. Finally, after some 30 minutes of strenuous effort, we had the fish alongside (John later confessed that he knew it was a big fish from the amount of line it ran away with when it took the bait). It proved to be a beautiful, shimmering yellow-finned tuna which took the three of us to lift it on board the boat. Back on shore we managed to hook it onto the large scales and weigh it. I weigh about 80kg and am 5'10" in height. The tuna was as long as I am tall and weighed over 100kg! How was that for beginner's luck? It was also a great day for the skipper, as he took it off to the fish market to sell.

This trip also marked an important change in my life. One day I was coming to the end of my gym exercise routine, and almost finishing on the last piece of equipment, the bike. I must have overdone things and blacked out for a few seconds and fell off the seat, but my feet were still held in the straps on the pedals. After a few minutes resting I felt all right apart from my leg being painful, having been held by the strap when I fell. I therefore went off to the SQU hospital on the campus and I was advised on exercises I should do to sort out the problem.

A few weeks later I decided to have a problem tooth removed, since medical care was free for me, apart from the approx. 50p payable by everyone for each visit to the hospital. The dentist agreed to take the tooth out but checked my blood pressure, which was sky high. She not only said she could not take out the tooth because she would have difficulty in stopping the bleeding afterwards, but insisted I went to see a doctor. I did and for a few weeks had my blood pressure monitored, and it remained high. The young Omani doctor therefore decided to put me on medication to lower it. None of this made any sense to me, because I was regularly exercising much more than I did in the UK, and eating much more healthily, with lots of fruit in my diet.

After 10 days my blood pressure was only slightly lower and she changed my medication. I was desperately concerned because Christmas was approaching and I was worried that I would be advised not to fly home to see my family. Fortunately I then saw a Finnish doctor, who was surprised that my medication had been changed, because he said it would take some time to kick in anyway. I was very relieved when he said I could go ahead with the trip home, and have a few drinks on the flight to relax me.

One thing I found odd was that all the medical staff in Oman only ever took one reading of my blood pressure, whereas in the UK three are taken, and the third can be significantly lower than the first. Perhaps the raised blood pressure was a consequence of all the problems I had encountered this time, particularly in the lab and organising the works visits, and the stress they caused.

I returned briefly to SQU at the beginning of January to mark the exam papers and complete my contract. On one of the modules (for which I was the module leader), when I reported the results to the exam board, the Head of the Department was placed in a quandary. The marks were so high that he was worried about defending them to the Dean of the Faculty of Science, to which I replied "just tell him it was the excellence of the teaching"! The rest of the staff agreed with me.

Oh, by the way, I did leave copies of my lecture notes behind!

CHAPTER 14

THE SULTANATE OF MUSCAT AND OMAN - A COUNTRY LIKE NO OTHER

My wife and I have been fortunate to travel extensively throughout the world. When our middle grandson recently asked her how many countries she had visited, she was amazed when the total came to 84! She had accompanied me to a couple of conferences relating to my work, in Munich in 1966 (during my PhD studies), and Hong Kong with one day in Shenzen in China in 1991. After the latter we added on a delightful holiday of one week in Bali followed by one on the neighbouring island of Lombok. Our globetrotting really started on the occasion of our silver wedding anniversary in 1988. Instead of buying each other presents we decided to have a long-haul holiday – as a one off–so we booked two weeks in the Maldives followed by a week in Singapore.

Our island in the Maldives was so small that we could walk right round it in 20 minutes, and it was delightful to be able to sunbathe and cool off in the Indian Ocean, with multitudes of brightly-coloured fish swimming just yards from the beach. Singapore was quite the opposite, with its hustle and bustle and lots to see. We were hooked, so a holiday to Hawaii followed the next year, and we have been going on long-distance holidays ever since.

We both agree that Oman is totally different from any other country we have visited, even though we had previously been to Dubai in the Middle East. The Sultanate of Muscat and Oman, to give it its full name, is bounded by the United Arab Emirates in the north, Saudi Arabia to the west and Yemen to the south and its coastline stretches for 1,000 miles along the Gulf of Oman towards the Indian Ocean. It is probably similar in size to Wales, but a significant area of the country is desert, in contrast to the coastal areas, and it has a population of about 2.5 million, although almost 25% are expatriate workers.

Sultan Qaboos, with the help of British forces, overthrew his father in 1970 when he was only 30 years old. He had been educated in England and studied at Sandhurst Royal Military Academy. Although an absolute ruler, he seemed to be universally liked by the people we met, and this was reflected in the lack of the disturbances which affected many other Middle Eastern countries during the 'Arab Spring' in 2015. A small one did occur in Sohar in the north of the country, but this soon petered out when the Sultan decreed that basic foodstuffs, like bread, were too expensive and that prices of these should be reduced by 10%. Within days they were!

The country has great wealth through its oil and gas reserves and it is amazing that there are such traffic jams in certain areas, considering the small population. However, due to very limited public transport, cars are essential. Although we met mostly professional people, who seemed very well off, we also met some much poorer people living in rural areas and some of these received food parcels every week. These were donated by the five or six extremely rich families who control most of the commerce, eg car dealerships.

Although a Muslim country, Oman probably lies between easy-going Dubai and very strict Saudi Arabia in its tolerance of non-Muslims, but it will gradually get more easy-going as its tourist trade continues to rapidly expand. Even when we were there it was rather bizarre to see in the shopping mall some Muslim women covered from head to toe with their burqas and only their eyes showing, and a few yards away Western women wearing little more than bikinis!

The climate is typically Middle Eastern with temperatures ranging from low 20°C in winter to over 40°C in summer and very little rainfall. In fact during our 18-month total stay there was less than a week's rain. However it can be torrential for a short time, with devastating consequences. The Harjar mountains that surround Muscat on the landward side are bare rock, so any rain just cascades straight off and the wadis (dried river beds) quickly become torrents. Each time this happens several people lose their lives by misjudging the force of the river and trying to drive through it in their 4x4s, which get washed away so that the passengers drown. On one occasion I was giving a colleague a lift to the airport (about 10 miles away) when the heavens opened and by the time we got there the water was up to the top of the car wheels. On the return journey I was driving steadily through the rain and noticed that a number of drivers were pulling off the road and stopping. Next day I mentioned this to an Omani colleague, and in all seriousness, she said that because they encounter rain so rarely a lot of drivers do not realise that they have to switch on their windscreen wipers!

What makes Oman so different and special is the dramatic scenery, ranging from lovely beaches to desert to high mountains (Jabal Sharms is the highest peak at over 3,000 metres or almost 10,000 feet) which surround its own version of the Grand Canyon, and even fjords, coupled with amazing statues, artefacts and historical sights. Virtually every town and village has these statues at the entrance, and examples are full-size prancing horses and even a full-sized dhow and fountains in the middle of a roundabout. Due to its position on some of the world's most important trade routes between Africa and Asia, well before the Middle Ages it was one of the richest parts of the world, due to its trade in Arabian horses and the purest frankincense. In the latter era their dhows travelled as far south as Zanzibar and east to India, competing for trade with the British and Portuguese. Hence there remain lots of forts and castles in the country.

The capital, Muscat, stretches for about 40 km along the northern coast, from the old city in the east to beyond the airport in the west, but it is only a narrow strip up to 10 km wide since it is hemmed in by the Harjar mountains. When we first visited there was only one dual carriageway along this route so the traffic was always heavy, but by our final visit a second one had opened, though it took a much longer route. There are a number of interesting sites by the first road, including the HQ of the National Bank with its gold doors, a fairly new Opera House and the magnificent Sultan Qaboos Mosque, plus sports stadia also bearing his name. However the place to start is the old city with the enormous and spectacular Sultan's palace (although he has two more in other parts of Oman) and lots of impressive Arab style buildings. Not too far from these is Mutrah, which has a delightful corniche from which you can regularly see one of the Sultan's opulent yachts berthed.

For us, and most people, the greater attraction is the souk and the gold souk, where I was able to improve my haggling skills. As well as cashmere scarves, all sorts of souvenirs are available and I was able to buy a lovely khanjar – the curved dagger worn by Omani males on special occasions. Further along the coast heading south was the marina from where I went on the fishing trip with John Williams. Known as Marina Bander, it has berths for many boats and also a restaurant, which not only sold alcohol but had a swimming pool and sun loungers which customers could use. We enjoyed these facilities on several weekends. On a cliff above it is the imposing British Ambassador's residence.

There is one part of Oman which is unique, and it is called Musandam. It is at the north-east tip of the Arabian Peninsula and only 20 miles across the Gulf of Hormuz from Iran. This is the stretch of water through which 90% of the world's crude oil passes in giant tankers. Musandam is totally surrounded by the United Arab Emirates. We flew there from Muscat (about an hour) for the weekend and the approach to the airport at Khasab was extremely hairy, with the wing tips of our small aircraft seeming to touch the mountains on either side as we came in to land. Fortunately take off for the return journey was out over the sea. Musandam is known as the 'Norway of the Middle East' because of its fjords and mountains, and cruise ships now dock there.

We enjoyed a dhow cruise around the coast and experienced a remarkable event. The skipper whistled and three dolphins immediately appeared and swam alongside the boat. Whilst watching fish being transferred from the fishing vessels to refrigerated vans in Khasab harbour, we were told that in a couple of hours they would be on sale in Dubai. After flying back to Muscat we were queuing to go through security and have our bags X-rayed at the airport when a young lady covered from head to toe in her black burqa just ignored security. She walked straight past it, and no one attempted to stop or question her!

Just a few hour's drive from the university, on the motorway which runs nearby, lies the ancient capital of Nizwa, a fine sight with its fort and souk and with several castles not far away. Just a few miles away the mountains also start to rise, and driving towards them we encountered a camel wandering alone along the roadside and nibbling at the bushes. The Al Hoota caves are worth a visit. At the time they had the only railway in Oman, which would take you from reception to the entrance, but it was not working during our visit.

There has been talk of building a train line from Muscat

down to Salalah in the south, a distance of 1,000 kilometres. We flew down to Salalah with friends one weekend but unfortunately they were ill, so all we saw was the hotel's beach. It is a popular place in the summer when temperatures soar, since it is cooled by moisture-laden winds from India. It is salutary to note that when Sultan Qaboos became ruler in 1970 there were only three primary schools and 10 kilometres of paved roads; now there are more than 10,000 kilometres, and over three million tourists visit the country each year. Clearly the fact that so many of the people speak English is a bonus for UK visitors.

At the start of the mountains we marvelled at a village where all the houses had been cut into the cliffs, and the people had built aqueducts to bring water down the mountains to irrigate their crops, such as pomegranate trees.

When my brother and his wife came to stay with us we hired a driver and Landcruiser for a three-day tour and visited many important tourist sites. These included the great sink hole, the last dhow building yard in Oman in Sur and Wadi Ban Khalid, where in its lagoons we could swim with the locals. We also spent some time on the sand dunes of the Wahiba Sands, where our driver showed his great skills; although the vehicle, of course, had four-wheel drive he never once needed to use it. Our original plan was to spend a night in a Bedouin tent in the desert, but this was

May and it was already so hot that even they had left the sands to move into neighbouring villages. Heading west from the sands is the Empty Quarter which stretches many miles across to Saudi Arabia and well into its interior; it was featured in the epic film *Lawrence of Arabia*.

However the highlight of our trip was a night excursion, to be guided by rangers and watch giant turtles laying their eggs, over 100 each. They had struggled up the beach and scooped out holes in the sand with their giant flippers. Already almost exhausted by the time that they had laid their eggs, they then moved a few yards away to scoop out another (false) hole or nest. This was to try and confuse the foxes, which love to eat the eggs and baby turtles.

So Oman is now well geared up for tourists with excellent air connections. Muscat Airport has been massively expanded in recent years and many more motorway quality roads built. In fact the motorway linking the airport to Muscat is lined by lots of beautiful greenery, flowers and shrubs, all of which require lots of water in the hot climate. Although some will come down from the mountains, most is obtained by desalination of sea water – a very costly process. All the major chains have had hotels there for many years and new golf courses are being built.

So for something different, try Oman.

CHAPTER 15

HOW CHEMISTRY TRANSFORMS OUR LIVES

Question – What do all of the following have in common? Computers, smart phones and electronic games; crease resistant, drip-dry clothes in virtually any colour; food that remains fresh for several days; life-saving drugs such as antibiotics, blood clot busting, blood pressure lowering and anticancer ones; and self-cleaning windows.

Answer – They all owe their existence to the contribution of chemistry and the chemical industry and there are many more examples.

The contribution of the chemical industry to the UK's financial health is enormous, with exports in 2014 exceeding

£60 billion, making it the country's largest manufacturing sector exporter. Over £60 million per day of added value (over £15 billion per year) was contributed to the UK's Gross Domestic Product. Growth in jobs exceeded 10%, with a total of over 70,000 in R&D alone. Of course the number of jobs supported is multiplied many times over when those in other areas which utilise the chemicals are included.

Despite these incredible achievements of chemistry and the chemical industry, they have always had an image problem. In fact 20 years ago their popular image was worse than that of the nuclear industry. Since then a greater awareness of environmental and green issues, plus a more open approach by the companies and greater interaction with their local communities, has led to a significant improvement in the public perception of the chemical industry. Two key drivers now are greener processes and sustainability. Greener processes have greater efficiency and produce far fewer waste products. This results in less loss of material in forming unwanted by-products and therefore leaves less material to dispose of, after suitable treatment. Both these benefits help to reduce costs, and the chemical industry has been very clever in finding uses for many by-products.

A simple example of greener and more environmentally acceptable products is paints. Many are now water based and have replaced the previously-used organic solvent-based ones. These advances have only been made possible by a big investment in research & development (R&D). Sustainability is the recognition that the Earth's resources are finite and therefore need to be used as efficiently as possible so that smaller amounts will suffice in any given situation. AstraZeneca measures the efficiency of using feedstocks by the Process Mass Intensity (PMI)[1], which is defined as Mass of all materials used in Processing divided by Mass of the Active Pharmaceutical Ingredient (API) Produced. The latter is the actual drug. Their Chemical Development Section in Macclesfield (where I had gained experience all those years ago, see Chapter 6), is committed to reducing the PMI for the manufacture of all new and existing drugs. One example is Avibactam, which is combined with β-lactam antibiotics to counter resistance in gram-negative bacteria. This started off with a PMI of 6,450, which meant that to make the daily dose of 1 gram of Avibactam would require 9.75 kilograms of material. To put it another way, to manufacture a patient's total course for 14 days would require 100 kilograms of material, an immense loss of material which has to be removed and either recycled, disposed of after treatment, or a use found for it. This was later marketed in combination with a different antibiotic, Ceftazidime, and by then the chemists had reduced the PMI down to 375. This resulted in a 90% reduction in the cost of materials, a lot less waste to dispose of and a shorter manufacturing time. Clearly this markedly improved profitability and is an excellent illustration of sustainability.

Despite this the public still has an automatic concern when 'chemicals' are mentioned – fanned by the media and newspapers only seeming to use the term when something has gone wrong, eg spillage or leaks of chemicals causing water pollution.

What the chemical industry does is to take a relatively small number of natural materials, such as crude oil, natural gas, limestone and salt, and turn them into a variety of chemical intermediates which are then converted into hundreds more chemicals. These in turn are made into finished products such as polystyrene, nylon and drugs. We only meet the chemicals as these finished products that we purchase from retailers. Note that the chemicals are obtained for the effects that they have.

We should appreciate that EVERYTHING IN THE WORLD IS COMPOSED OF CHEMICALS, even ourselves. To live and breathe a multitude of complex chemical reactions go on in our bodies, eg enzymes breaking down our food to provide us with nutrients and energy. In order to gain a balanced insight into the benefits that chemistry and the chemical industry have brought us, as well as some of the problems and disasters, let's start with the latter, then consider the former and finally visit a few areas where the jury is still out, with arguments for and against, eg GM crops and organic foods.

The first report on the adverse effect of chemicals on the environment to receive widespread publicity was about a pesticide known as DDT. This chemical compound had been known since 1873, but it only came into prominence in 1939 when Paul Muller of Geigy showed that it could be used to control insect pests, particularly malaria-carrying mosquitoes. Within a few years of this discovery, during the Second World War, it was used by the US Army in Naples to halt the spread of a typhus epidemic for the first time ever.

In the 1950s malaria was killing over a million people a year just in India. Within a few years, following extensive use of DDT, this had dropped to a thousand a year. Spraying onto the mosquitoes' breeding grounds, particularly stagnant pools, throughout tropical countries soon led to a similar worldwide decline in mortality rates. The possible adverse environmental effects of DDT were highlighted in 1962 in the book *Silent Spring*, written by the biologist Rachel Carson. Research over several years established that the DDT was absorbed in fatty tissues of many living species. This would not have been a problem, but it was discovered that the DDT became more concentrated in these tissues as it passed up the food chain. The result was that low levels were detected in fish (where it did not cause any problems) but when the fish were eaten by birds, and DDT passed further up the food chain and eventually to birds of prey, it had reached levels as high as 5000 parts per million. This did cause serious problems, including, in some cases, death of the birds, and led to calls for DDT to be banned, which it eventually was. Interestingly, during the court hearings which led to this, executives from some of the manufacturing companies publicly ate a few grams a day of DDT (foolishly) just to demonstrate how safe it was for humans. By this time DDT was becoming less effective anyway due to the build-up of resistance in the mosquitoes.

This chain of events is interesting in the light of the fact that when DDT's activity was first discovered it seemed to be almost the perfect insecticide because it had high activity against a wide range of insect pests, had little or no mammalian toxicity, was easily and cheaply made and was very stable. This final property seemed a great virtue because it meant that it would hang around for a long time, killing many insect pests. Ironically it proved DDT's undoing, because it was its great stability that allowed it to remain unchanged as it passed up the food chain.

It is important to note that until Rachel Carson's comments no one had really appreciated that chemicals might cause adverse environmental effects. This was of great personal interest to me for two reasons. Firstly I used it in my specialist lecture course on the agrochemical industry, and secondly an aspect of my research work was making entirely new compounds that might exhibit pesticidal activity. Several that we made did show activity during the initial screening trials, but when the concentration was reduced to commercially-acceptable levels the activity disappeared.

In 1961 there was a similar situation with the thalidomide tragedy. This drug was prescribed as a sedative, and later to ease the symptoms of morning sickness in pregnant women. Sadly this resulted in many of them giving birth to children with terrible deformities of their limbs. The companies involved, Chemie Grunenthal and Distillers, could not be blamed for not detecting this side effect during the drug's discovery and development because, at the time, no one believed that any drug could pass from the mother to the embryo in the womb. Naturally, since that discovery, this is one of the tests which are carried out very early in the development of any potential new drugs. Where these companies were badly at fault was in the time that they took to withdraw the drug from the market, even though more and more reports from doctors were highlighting the problems.

Let us now consider the two worst-ever disasters in the chemical industry, at Flixborough in England (1974) and Bhopal in India (1984). Nypro UK's plant at Flixborough was producing Nylon 6 precursors, and one of the reactors had been temporarily removed for repair, being replaced by a large diameter pipe, which was inadequately supported. As a result, leakage of highly flammable cyclohexane occurred, producing a very large cloud of gas which eventually ignited, causing a massive explosion. This resulted in 28 deaths and 100 people injured, along with damage to nearly 200 factories, shops and houses in the neighbourhood. The explosion was so big because of the large amount of flammable material at the plant – several hundred tons. This was a consequence of the process's inefficiency; only 6% of the material fed to the reactor was actually consumed in making the product and all the rest had to be recovered and recycled.

The disaster at Bhopal was by far the chemical industry's worst ever, and some of the repercussions continue even today. The plant was making the insecticide Carbaryl, which is highly active against a very wide range of insect pests and also has a very low mammalian toxicity. The name perhaps reflects that of the company making it, Union Carbide, which was a US multinational and one of the largest chemical companies in the world.

One of the chemicals used in the process was methyl isocyanate (MIC), which is a very reactive and toxic material. It reacts strongly with water at room temperature and the reaction is strongly exothermic, ie it generates a lot of heat. Tragically a plant operative opened the wrong valve, which allowed water into a large tank of MIC. This immediately started a violent reaction producing lots of heat and a rapid build-up of pressure in the sealed tank. This caused the bursting disc to break, allowing a deadly cloud of MIC to be released into the atmosphere and over many homes which stood right next to the factory. The MIC should have passed through scrubbers containing sodium hydroxide solution, where a chemical reaction would have rendered it relatively harmless. Sadly the scrubbers were not working that day. As a result of this chain of events, well over 3000 people eventually lost their lives, with many more suffering (some still even today) serious respiratory problems.

This toll was so high for two reasons: firstly the proximity to the factory of so many houses and secondly, absolutely disgracefully, the fact that company officials did not reveal to the medical teams what the chemical was until a few days later. In 1989, five years after the disaster, the Indian Government, on behalf of the victims, accepted Union Carbide's final offer of $470 million in compensation, while the company had also previously financed the building of a hospital to treat the victims. The company has since sold the factory and the site.

When we analyse these disasters it is clear that the cause of both was human error. At Flixborough it was the failure to ensure that the pipe was correctly supported and at Bhopal it was the opening of the wrong valve, plus the failure to ensure that the scrubbers were working.

Turning back to environmental issues, one in which I had a personal interest (see Chapter 10) was the CFCs (chlorofluorocarbons). These had been hailed as wonder products when they were first discovered by Midgely in the 1930s, the reasons being that they were (a) non-toxic, (b) non-flammable and (c) chemically unreactive or inert. This led to their large-scale use as refrigerants (where they replaced highly toxic ammonia or hydrogen sulphide), foam-blowing agents and what the public knows them best for – aerosol propellants.

In 1974 Roland and Molina suggested that because of their great stability they could rise unchanged into the stratosphere. That on its own would not have been a problem, but the speculation was that at this altitude the short wavelength (high energy) UV-B rays would be powerful enough to break the carbon-chlorine bonds in the CFCs and produce reactive free radicals. These in turn would attack the ozone molecules and destroy them. Even worse, just one free radical could destroy many ozone molecules.

Why would this matter? The ozone layer in the stratosphere protects us on Earth from these dangerous UV-B rays and any reduction in this layer would result in a big increase in the number of cases of skin cancer.

It was to be another 20 years before these theories were confirmed. One of the major difficulties was that the ozone layer shrinks and expands throughout the year naturally, particular over Antarctica, so assigning how much of the change was due to nature and how much to the effects of CFCs was difficult. Measurements were only possible after the invention of equipment to do this from the ground or from aircraft, since the stratosphere is some 10-50 kilometres above the Earth's surface. However this led to the first-ever international agreement on an environmental issue, the Montreal Protocol, in 1987. Some 50 nations signed up to this and thereby pledged to reduce the use of CFCs and phase them out as soon as possible. Due to their widespread and important uses replacements would have to be found and developed first. Britain, with the Prime Minister, Margaret Thatcher driving it, wanted this to happen very quickly. However a project of this scale would normally take 10-20 years to complete. In order to speed things up enormous resources were committed by companies like ICI and also DuPont in the USA. This was how I became involved at ICI, as described in chapter 10.

Since the chlorine in the CFC molecules was the problem, research focused on similar molecules, but ones that did not contain chlorine. These were the HFCs (hydrofluorocarbons), or HFAs (hydrofluoroalkanes) as the industry prefers to call them, since 'HFC' is a bit close to

'CFC' and the associated bad publicity. These HFCs have much shorter atmospheric lifetimes, so they tend to break down before they can reach the stratosphere, and therefore do not get a chance to attack the ozone molecules. They would be unable to anyway since they do not contain chlorine.

This mammoth R&D effort enabled the new products to be manufactured within the amazingly short timetable of just five years from the research commencing. It required innovative approaches, such as involving the engineers, who would design the manufacturing plant, very early in the project instead of the then current practice of very late on. Also, and very unusually, there was excellent inter-company collaboration on joint environmental and toxicity studies.

Note the parallel with DDT here, where the downfall of the CFCs was also, ironically, due to their great chemical stability, which was also deemed very advantageous when they were first discovered.

As I write (2017), replacements for HFCs in turn are now being sought because of their contribution to global warming.

We have now considered a few terrible disasters from the chemical industry which, quite rightly, received widespread publicity. However these must be looked at in context. Throughout the world hundreds of thousands of chemical processes are operated every day, with some of the larger plants eg petrochemical plants (those producing chemicals from oil and natural gas) and ammonia plants operating 24 hours per day and 365 days per year, except for planned maintenance. Many operate at high temperatures and pressures and also use toxic chemicals. How often do we hear or read about any problems with them? Only very occasionally, so we should admire their work and be proud that the vast majority of these plants are operated in an efficient and safe manner.

We have also looked at environmental and safety issues concerning insecticides and the drug thalidomide. With DDT and thalidomide the harmful effects could not have been predicted and therefore could not be picked up in the testing programme. However, although it took time, they were withdrawn from use and replaced by newer, improved products which did not cause these problems. Tests to detect these problems are now standard procedures in the discovery and development of new drugs and pesticides. These issues are taken up later in this chapter.

So what have we got to thank the chemical industry for?

Quite simply, life as we experience it. In fact we would still be living in the Dark Ages without the research and development producing so many new products. As already mentioned, we do not see chemicals as such but only the end products they have been made into, eg paint, nylon and polyester clothing dyed with synthetic pigments to produce whatever colour we wish. Oh, by the way, there would be no computers or smart phones without the contribution of R&D in chemistry. There is an immense number of products to choose from to look at in more detail, but I will limit myself to automobiles, drugs and pesticides and outline the amazing advances in each of these areas.

With cars, an immediate example is service intervals. Back in the late 1960s my cars, such as the Mark 1 Ford Cortina, needed servicing every 3,000 miles, whereas my present vehicle, a Hyundai I30, only needs it every 20,000 miles. This remarkable improvement is due partly to advances in engine technology but also to the development of better, more stable and therefore longer lasting lubricating oils. Years ago even after just 1,000 miles the engine oil had turned black, whereas checking my current oil, even after more than 17,000 miles it is only slightly darker than the original golden-brown colour. Rusting of the metal car bodywork, even after just a few years, was not uncommon but is now rare due to anti-corrosion treatment and the high-quality acrylic paint finishes. The result is that the warranty period has increased in many cases from one to five to seven years. We are also aware of the better quality, more environmentally-acceptable fuels, such as unleaded petrol.

Before looking at specific examples of drugs and pesticides, there are a few general points to understand.

Firstly, none of these products will ever be totally free of side effects, so a judgement has to be made on the value of the benefits against the unwanted side effects. Secondly, no product can ever be guaranteed totally safe. What the industry seeks to do is to discover and develop new products with greater potency and selectivity and fewer side effects. Having rightly, over the last few decades, insisted on more extensive testing of potential new drugs and pesticides, we now need to achieve a balance because ever more testing is being imposed, most of which will make very little (if any) difference to the product's safety. The consequences are the poorer success rates leading to the increasing length of time and cost of developing each new product.

How long does it take, and cost, just to get one new product onto the market? The answer is a staggering 12 years, at a cost of over £1 billion on average.

Typically the testing programme starts with some 25,000 compounds (most of them entirely new and made by the company's synthetic chemists and university researchers). By the end of the 12 years of testing, 24,999 will have been rejected and only one will reach the market. The cost of testing all these rejects is what pushes the final figure so high. Probably 50% of the candidates are, fortunately, rejected in the first few years of testing. Clearly therefore the company would want to identify the ones which are not going to make it as early in the testing programme as possible, because the tests become more expensive as the programme proceeds, with each individual test costing as much as £500,000 in the final stages of testing. A patent on the product typically runs for 15 years and up to half of this period may have been lost during the testing programme, so this leaves a very short period for patent-protected sales without competition during which the company can try to recoup the enormous R&D costs and start to make a profit. Deciding when to apply for a patent is a tricky decision, because the information then enters the public domain and other companies can see what you are working on and decide whether to compete with you or make something which is slightly different and also shows activity. This might allow them to get round the patent. Once the patent runs out, other companies can start making generic versions and selling them cheaply, because they have had none of the enormous R&D costs.

Is it any wonder that the company holding the patent needs, and wants, to charge high prices?

The increasing cost of developing new drugs has already had serious consequences. Just as bacteria are getting resistant to most of our large array of antibiotics, most of the giant pharmaceutical companies have almost ceased developing new ones, because it is unlikely that they will ever recover the enormous R&D costs. This has become a worldwide issue and in the UK, companies, the Government and organisations like the Gates foundation are coming together to fund new discovery work. Developments like anti-cancer drugs are a much more appealing, and potentially more profitable, target. Nevertheless, the R&D spend each year is incredibly high, with several of the multinational pharma giants spending over $1 billion. In the UK alone £4 billion was invested in 2013.

Considering the pharmaceutical industry only really developed after 1945, it has made a remarkable contribution to our health and wellbeing. In 1900, boys' life expectancy was 48 and 52 for girls; the corresponding figures for 2015 were 79 and 83. Clearly improved hygiene and nutrition have made important contributions, but so has the pharmaceutical industry with medicines such as antibiotics and vaccines. So much so that many killer diseases like diphtheria, smallpox and TB have been almost eliminated, although in the last few years there has been a significant increase in the number of TB cases in countries like Russia. The efficacy of penicillin and more recent antibiotics has saved billions of lives, but unnecessary use, and failure to complete the course prescribed, has led to very serious resistance and reduced their effectiveness. In fact, unless something is done quickly, pessimists are predicting a return to the dark days before we had antibiotics when even small cuts could lead to septicaemia and, in some cases, death.

How many people take daily medication to prevent heart attacks, or to lower blood pressure, or even keep you alive?

The answer is an increasing number, particularly the elderly. I am sure that we all have family members falling into this category. My sister-in-law has diabetes and has to daily inject insulin, made by the pharmaceutical industry. In my own case I am taking tablets to reduce my blood pressure and therefore reduce the chance of a heart attack or stroke, since my doctor calculated that there is a 20% of this happening in my lifetime. I take Ramipril and Amlodipine and, as a precaution, Simvastatin to ensure my cholesterol level remains low. The latter is one of the group of statins which several million people in this country alone take each day for the same reason, although there are some dissenters in the medical profession regarding their benefits, and some people have suffered unpleasant side effects. Statins cost only a few pence per tablet, whereas anti-cancer drugs can cost over £1,000 for just a few tablets.

Interestingly, in October 2016 I was at one of our SCI Public Lectures in London given by Sir Simon Campbell on "Drug Discovery". He had led the team at Pfizer which discovered both Amlodipine and Viagra. The latter is very well known as a treatment for erectile dysfunction. It was originally being developed as an improvement on Amlodipine for reducing blood pressure. An independent company was reporting back to Pfizer on the clinical trials which they had carried out for them. Everything was coming out negative, but fortunately the trials had been carried out on students, and as an aside at the end of the report, it was disclosed that one of them reported getting an erection when he took the tablet. Thus, although the product was no good for its planned use, it became a $1 billion per annum blockbuster.

I am sure that you can think of many other drugs and medicines that are vital to us, eg flu vaccinations, anti-malarials and anti-cancer ones.

Despite their adverse publicity in a few cases, pesticides have made an outstanding contribution to increasing the yields of growing crops, usually by reducing the amounts consumed by pests, be they fungi, insects or weeds. Each year there is increasing pressure to grow more crops for food (and increasingly for biofuels), but this is getting more and more difficult since the total land available is decreasing as unproductive areas of land, like deserts, expand. The situation is exacerbated because the number of mouths to feed is increasing rapidly, with the world's population predicted to reach over nine billion by 2025.

Another range of products produced by the chemical industry has also helped to dramatically improve yields, namely artificial fertilisers. These are based on ammonia, phosphates and potash, which provide the nutrients nitrogen, phosphorus and potassium, which all plants need to grow. Millions of tons are manufactured each year and modern intensive farming would be impossible without them. However there have been some adverse environmental effects, where excess fertiliser has run off the fields into rivers and watercourses, causing problems such as excess algal growth.

The improvement in yields as a result of the above, plus better farming practice, has been remarkable. For the three main global cereals (maize, rice and wheat), between 1915 and 2015 the increase was over 500%, and since 1960 alone over 100%.

Focusing on pesticides (or 'plant growth regulators', as the industry prefers to call them for obvious reasons) we have seen remarkable improvements in activity (so less needs using) and selectivity (so the product only attacks the desired pest and should be less likely to cause any environmental problems). The reduction in application rates for herbicides is typically down from several kgs/hectare to 0.01 kgs/hectare and for pyrethrin insecticides from 0.1 kg/hectare to a tiny 0.01 kgs/hectare. A hectare of land measures 100 x 100 metres, which is equivalent to two full-sized football pitches side by side. You have probably exploited the selectivity of herbicides by watering them onto your lawn, where they kill broad-leaved weeds like dandelions and daisies but leave the grass untouched. The active chemicals are usually compounds known as 2, 4-D or

MCPA, and these are active at a level of 100 parts per million, so just 50 grams spread over the whole pitch at Wembley stadium would kill off all the broad-leaved weeds. Interestingly, at much lower doses still these chemicals are used in Hawaii to stimulate pineapple plants to flower for the benefit of the tourists.

Another well-known weed killer is Paraquat, although this is a total solution, killing all green plants. Hence we use it to remove weeds growing on paths or patios, whilst the farmer applies it after harvesting to clear the ground before planting the next crop. This eliminates the need for ploughing. Concerns about it have recently led to it being banned in some countries.

The pyrethrin insecticides are the active materials in the knockdown sprays used to kill flies, wasps etc. in flight. You can tell that they act on the insects' nervous system when you see the flies on their backs swinging madly around. Several thousand pesticides have been approved for use in the UK, following extensive scrutiny of all the test results by Government bodies, so when one or two are cited as causing problems then the scientific evidence should be carefully reviewed, and if proven, the pesticide should be banned and replaced, but we should view this in context.

Over the last 20 years some exciting non-chemical methods of insect control have been developed, including release of sterilized males, use of biological predators, microbial (or living) insecticides and growth-regulating hormones. To date however, they have only captured a small share of the market, and they tend to be used in special situations, eg in greenhouses.

We should be grateful to the agrochemical industry for protecting us from historical calamities such as the biblical plagues of locusts and the Irish potato famine in 1840, where the crop was destroyed by being infected with a fungus known as potato blight and as a result 100,000 people died. A gigantic swarm of locusts (up to 2 million) can eat 10,000 tons of green crops in a day. Fortunately biologists can now predict when the swarms are likely to form, and the insects can then be sprayed with an insecticide and killed while still on the ground.

Let us conclude this chapter by looking at two areas where there is debate for and against – organic foods, and GM (genetically modified) crops.

The term 'organic foods' is absurd, since it is meant to describe only foodstuffs that have been grown naturally, without the use of artificial fertilisers or pesticides. However all foods, and indeed all living things, are organic, since the term describes chemical compounds of, or containing, carbon and that is what all life is made of. It is claimed that 'organic compounds' taste better and are more nutritious, allowing the producers to charge a higher price for them. Although there may be strong support for the former claim, recent research has shown that for some products the non-organic version is actually more nutritious. Clearly the choice is down to the individual's taste. However we in the affluent parts of the world are fortunate to have this choice and since the yields of 'organic' products are significantly lower than those produced using artificial fertilisers and pesticides, there is no way that going over entirely to them could possibly supply enough food, and the number of people currently starving would undoubtedly increase significantly.

There has been even more controversy, for many years, over GM crops, with such strong opposition in the UK that even trials have yet to be carried out. Yet for a number of years most of the enormous quantities of cereals grown in the USA have been GM varieties, and despite the concerns of the protesters, there do not seem to have been any particular problems with the production and eating of them. As already mentioned, the dramatic increase in yields of rice owes a lot to the introduction of genetically-modified strains. Clearly the only way to resolve matters and allay concerns is to carry out carefully-controlled trials, analyse the results, and then come to a conclusion based on the scientific facts that have emerged.

Hopefully you have now been convinced that despite some problems (in reality very few), the contribution of chemistry and the chemical industry to our lives has been massively beneficial.

CHAPTER 16

LOOKING BACK ON A FULL LIFE

I have written this book because I feel I have had an interesting life and want to share details of my experiences and show what can be achieved with determination and really hard work. It has certainly been unusual in respect of my career, where the route into it was very different from that normally taken by academics, and bearing in mind the low starting point in terms of GCEs acquired, the achievements have been amazing. So how do I reflect on it so far, since I hope it has many more years to run?

I feel fortunate to have been born in the middle of the 20th century, because otherwise, as the life expectancy data in chapter 15 suggest, I would almost certainly have died many years ago and not been able to give an account of my 74 years and counting. Although my father and his brother both died in their sixties after suffering illness for several years, my mother's side of the family have been noted for living to ripe old ages. Her grandma lived into her 90s, and died then only after having her leg amputated because of gangrene and failing to recover afterwards. Her mother lived to be 94. Despite being petite, my mother looked after my father, who was six feet and over 16 stone, throughout his illnesses. He suffered from high blood pressure (and had to take warfarin to thin his blood) and later from Parkinson's disease. Several times when he had fallen out of bed or was stuck in the shower, she managed to get him sorted, but blamed her later suffering from angina on this. When they lived near us in Heswall I would go over at the weekends to give him a good wash in the shower. As he became less fit they took the decision to move to Radcliffe-on-Trent, where my brother lived. They again purchased their own flat in a complex and attached to it was a nursing home, where my father could live when he was not well enough to continue living at home. This he did for a short time before he passed away.

Mum continued to look after herself in the flat, even cooking for herself well into her eighties. The cooking was a big worry for all of us, because her eyesight was failing badly, since she had macular degeneration, which made it difficult for her to see the cooker controls. We were all delighted when she started getting ready-made meals delivered and she only had to warm them in the microwave. In addition, on our monthly visits my wife Joy would take her 10 lovely roast dinners, which she had cooked and frozen. Not surprisingly at her age, Mum grew increasingly forgetful, but the great thing was that she could laugh about it and at herself.

As she turned 90 we noted that she found it increasingly difficult to look after herself, but we did not want to push her into going into a residential home. We were therefore delighted in 2014 when she made the decision herself. The home was only a very short distance from her flat and she already knew some of the residents, so she fitted in easily and well, soon persuading several of them to go with her to her afternoon clubs at the local British Legion. She really enjoyed being looked after at 96 years old.

We often joked with her about her receiving a telegram from the Queen when she was 100 years old. Being confident that this would happen, we were shocked when a few months into 2015, she contracted pneumonia, and sadly passed away on the 16th April. Her family was the most important thing in her life and she was the one who made us so closely knit. The role of matriarch has now passed, on my side of the family, to Joy, who Mum always said was "the glue that keeps the family together". I hope I have inherited her longevity genes.

I have been blessed in several ways, most of which relate to my family. Firstly I was born to parents who were tremendously caring, loving and supportive. My father did not always make this obvious, for example, when I wanted to borrow the car he always had comments to make first, which could have been taken as meaning he was not keen, but he always did loan it to me. It was often easier just to put the request to Mum. Secondly, as is apparent from comments throughout this book, my wife Joy has been immensely supportive, caring and looking after me very well. She is an excellent cook and home-maker, having built these attributes on the teachings of her mother, and she has in turn passed them onto our children and grandchildren. Now she is starting again with our great-granddaughter Alyssa, who although only two, is already enjoying learning to bake. Joy has taught our granddaughter Abby, aged nine, as well as our grandsons Liam, Archie and Sam, how to bake, cook, sew and knit.

I've also been grateful for my ability to grasp opportunities as they came my way and build on them, and to overcome adversity when it has reared its head. I suppose the first opportunity was being offered the chance to go on the sandwich course at college. Clearly the chance to carry out research for a PhD degree, when we hardly knew what it entailed, was a big opportunity and, as we have seen, it shaped the rest of my life. It was a big decision to leave a salaried position as a research chemist and live on a student grant, since my wife was no longer working following the birth of our son Simon. Keith Whittles approaching me to write textbooks was another example, and though it brought me lots of "blood, sweat and tears", it was not only enjoyable and very satisfying, but it enhanced my career and standing in the chemical community.

The opportunity to become a Visiting Consultant at Sultan Qaboos University in Oman probably arose, as I surmised in chapter 13, because of my books and my reputation. John Williams taking me fishing there and catching that enormous 100 kg yellow-finned tuna was magical, but also sad as the great creature's incandescent blue and green scales gradually dulled, despite the skipper regularly pouring water over the skin, as we sailed back to port.

It is obvious that sport did, and still does, play an important part in my life and looking back probably the greatest achievements were when I was at Middlesbrough High School and won the town 100 metres sprint (though I was certainly no Usain Bolt in the making), the school tennis championship, and played for the school cricket team. Topping them all though was captaining the school rugby team and playing all 3 matches for my county of North Yorkshire.

In retirement, as mentioned previously, my neighbour had introduced me and two of our other friends firstly to golf and later to crown green bowls. He soon tired of golf, but another friend and I continued to play (as I still do) until he recently had to give it up due to ill health. We had all become friends when we were founder members of Neston Swimming Club in our home town and served on the committee.

For many years all four of us played for the teams of Neston Royal British Legion Crown Green Bowling club, with some of us serving as team captains and Chair. In 1990 my golfing partner moved to Greasby, where he joined the local bowls club, Royden Hall. I stayed with Neston until 1990, when I resigned as Chairman and moved to Heswall Royal British Legion, a higher-level club. During our time at Neston we won several cups and leagues, and I had one memorable year in 2002 in individual competitions. Firstly I won through to the finals (last 16 out of an entry of 100-plus) of the Bebington Handicap. Despite playing against the stars from the leagues on the Wirral, I won my first two games to reach the semi-final. There I encountered an established county player and was slightly off my excellent form of the previous two matches but still gave a good account, losing 21-17. My opponent went on to win the final and lift the cup. For my efforts I received £20 in prize money.

I also entered the Ellesmere Port and Neston Pioneer Cup, which was played at the Conservative Club green in

Ellesmere Port. Having battled my way through to the final I now faced an opponent playing on his home green – a big advantage. Early on he played very well, especially on his favoured corner-to-corner long marks. With his family cheering him on he went 19-10 up, which meant he only needed two shots for victory. However, as described when I won the school tennis championship, one of my great virtues is that I never give up, no matter how hopeless the situation seems. I won the jack and immediately changed to a short mark with lots of swing (a common tactic) and gradually pulled him back. There were lots of oohs and aahs, plus near misses, before I eventually triumphed by the narrowest of margins, 21-20! My reward was a nice large cup (to hold for a year) plus £25 prize money.

Some of my best results in recent years have been in mixed doubles competitions, where my relaxed and encouraging nature seems to bring out the best in my partners. In our first season, in 2013, with my (now) regular partner, who is a member of the ladies' section at Heswall, I reached the semi-finals of two big local competitions, namely the Cammell Lairds and Pensby open events, which both attracted over 50 pairs of bowlers from across the Wirral and as far away as Stafford. As a result we were each some £50 better off. Since then we have won a couple of our own club competitions and I have won three more, each with different partners.

Playing four times a week for three different Heswall teams (and captaining one of the two veterans' teams) is quite a commitment, but a very enjoyable one. The season lasts from Easter to late September. For the last 10 years I have also been a member of The Oaks Golf Club at Mollington (near Chester), taking part in the seniors competition on a Wednesday. Although I could generally manage only every other week, it was very enjoyable, because they were a good bunch and very friendly. In the summer I invariably had to rush straight from the course to go and play bowls for one of my veterans' teams. Sadly in May 2016 the club was disbanded when the course owners accepted an offer from a development company. Since then I have lost my enthusiasm and have only played a few rounds. However if I can get my wife to start playing again I am sure I will be back, as keen as ever!

So I have had some successes in local crown green bowling competitions – and I hope I am not finished yet! It is also very satisfying that my family members have inherited this love of sport; in their case the number one interest is football. My son, Simon (and son-in-law Les), plus eldest grandson, Liam, and youngest one, Sam, have all done well playing at the local level, with our only granddaughter, Abby, competing at cross-country for her primary school, whilst our middle grandson, Archie, is a very good swimmer. Both Liam and Simon were chosen as the 'Players' Player of the Year' in their respective leagues, a tremendous accolade. We are waiting to see what takes our first great grandchild, Alyssa's, fancy. Simon, his wife Sarah, and I also enjoy hill and mountain walking. Liam, Les, Simon, Joy and I all enjoy golf.

For the foreseeable future I will continue to serve on learned body committees and promote chemistry and science to young people, and to promote the great benefits of chemistry and the chemical industry, whilst acknowledging the few problems which have arisen.

However the most important part of my life will continue to be my family. Simon and Susan have both followed me into teaching, albeit in schools. Simon is Director of Sixth Form Studies at a very large comprehensive school, whilst Susan has taught part-time in a primary school since the birth of her daughter, Abby. Simon's sons Archie and Sam and Susan's son Liam, plus daughter Abby, and Liam's daughter Alyssa, complete our side of the Heaton family. Since Simon's family live within an hour's drive of us and the remaining family members live locally, we get together as a family regularly, for a meal (usually cooked by Granny Joy), or to do something together.

So throughout my career I have had great support from my parents, then my wife, and then my family, and I have been fortunate to look forward to going to work because I really enjoyed what I was doing. Looking back to where I started from and what I achieved in my academic career seems just amazing; going from academic failure at school (while being the only fifth former to win the Old Boys' Cup), studying in college (winning the ICI prize as the Best Science Student), gaining my PhD and becoming Lecturer, Senior Lecturer, Reader and finally Professor of Chemical Education as well as Head of Chemistry. Along the way I have written textbooks, run international conferences, chaired international committees and been awarded SCI's prestigious Lampitt Medal.

My life has been remarkable, and long may it continue! Perhaps my title and all the letters I have earned the right to put after my name sum up my achievements: Professor Alan Heaton, PhD, EurChem, CChem, CSci, FRSC, SCIMem (Doctor of Philosophy, European Chemist, Chartered Chemist, Chartered Scientist, Fellow of the Royal Society of Chemistry, SCI Member.)

Reference

1. Measuring Sustainability, Chemistry and Innovation, 2016, pages 26-29. Special Issue of Chemistry and Industry.

www.ingramcontent.com/pod-product-compliance
Lightning Source LLC
Chambersburg PA
CBHW022114040426
42450CB00006B/701